MY JOURNEY
TO FREEDOM

PRAISE FOR *MY JOURNEY TO FREEDOM*

Erika's story is both moving and meaningful. It is a testimony to the grace of God in every season. Through deep valleys and new beginnings, she offers wisdom, strength, and hope. I pray her words encourage you to trust God's hand even when you can't see His plan.

— **PASTOR LISA YOUNG**, Fellowship Church

I am blessed to call Erika my friend and have watched her grow and heal, becoming a powerful role model and encouragement to so many. Her story of faith, courage, love, and never giving up on herself or her daughter is an incredible testimony of God's faithfulness and protection. Erika is a huge blessing to all who know and come to know her through her ministry, writing, and friendship.

— **KIRSTEN JOHNSON**, Director at *The Road Adventure*

From her teen years to today, Erika's journey is a powerful testimony of courage, faith, and perseverance. Her unshakable determination to protect herself and her daughter, and her relentless pursuit of truth, inspire everyone who knows her. Erika's warmth, charm, and extraordinary strength shine through every page. *My Journey to Freedom* is more than a memoir—it is a lifeline of hope for every parent walking the path of raising a child alone.

— **LISA FAHEY** Author, *Simply, Rise Up, Women of God, Restored,* You Are Loved, and *Just As You Are*

As Erika's attorney, I witnessed her suffering at a very low point in her life. Nothing causes a parent more stress and anxiety than a threat to their child's safety and well-being. Witnessing her ascension from the depths of this despair to a thriving woman of faith has been my privilege. I have watched Erika emerge from her trials and tribulations largely through helping others navigate life's challenges. Her story is inspiring and relatable, and she has used her experiences to make a positive impact in the world.

— **POLLY O'TOOLE**, Attorney at Law

To say that I am proud to call Erika one of my very best friends would be an understatement. She is that friend who never gave up on me, while seeing me so much better than I saw myself, and she continues to shine her light into me as well as literally everyone she meets! The fact that she has stepped into courage and allowed herself to be vulnerable while sharing her journey is beyond exciting. We cheer each other on and continue to be blown away by God's blessings. We are no longer surprised by the doors that swing wide open, and we step into them with gratitude, our heads up and our hearts open! What an exciting gift that Erika has put her story down on paper. She created this memoir to highlight her journey, her redemption, and her trials and triumphs to showcase God's Amazing Grace! Respectfully Cheering LOUDLY!

— SHELLEY GOAD (Good) BS BHS, LCDC

My childhood friend Erika, with the spunk of Punky Brewster and a smile that could light the darkest day, journeyed from the clay hills of "The Pearl" and the hallways of the City of Champions to her place of purpose in the Black Hills of South Dakota. Along the way, she faced despair, heartbreak, and enough drama to fuel a Netflix series—yet she emerged stronger, smiling, and looking fabulous. Erika has turned her pain into power, and she's here to help you laugh, cry, and strut your way to the other side of your own struggles. Take this journey with her—you won't regret it.

— KEATON FUDGE, Pastor

There is nothing like a supernatural God-story to encourage me to keep praying, keep believing, keep hoping in a God who answers the deep cries of our heart. Erika's book is one of those stories. To know her now and to read what was, almost seems like fiction. Her life is a testament of a woman who kept believing in the goodness and power of god and is now experiencing the joy of answered prayer. If you're in the middle of hell on earth, read this book. You will hear yourself saying, "If God did that for Erika, He can do it for me."

— BECKY HENNESY, Pastor, Trinity Church Cedar Hill, Texas

MY JOURNEY TO FREEDOM

A MEMOIR OF FAITH AND GOD'S AMAZING GRACE

ERIKA SEAMAYER-WILLIAMSON

Farmhouse Publishings

For information on distribution rights, royalties, derivative works, or licensing opportunities on behalf of this content or work, please contact the publisher at the address below:

Farmhouse Publishings, LLC
P.O. Box 333
Spearfish, SD 57783

Scripture quotations marked (NIV) are taken from THE HOLY BIBLE, NEW INTERNATIONAL VERSION®. Copyright© 1973, 1978, 1984, 2011 by Biblica, Inc.™. Used by permission of Zondervan.

Although the author and publisher have tried to ensure that the information and advice in this book were correct and accurate at press time, the author and publisher do not assume and disclaim any liability to any party for any loss, damage, or disruption caused by acting upon the information in this book or by errors or omissions, whether such errors or omissions result from negligence, accident, or any other cause.

ISBN (Softcover): 979-8-9996472-4-5
ISBN (Hardcover): 979-8-9996472-5-2
ISBN (Ebook): 979-8-9996472-6-9

Design by Heidi Caperton
Editing by Kendra Paulton

Printed in the United States of America

To my daughter, Chelsea Laine, and her beautiful
daughter, my granddaughter Livy, whose laughter, love,
and courage carried me through the darkest storms.

To my precious husband, Erik, whose love and
encouragement made this book possible.

To Erik's children and their families—Brennan & Sarah, and Talia,
Mila and Max, Preston and Chandler, and Dylan & Savannah,
and Wrenley and Hallie—you are a blessing to my life.

To my mother, Kay Seamayer, who faithfully stood by my side—
sitting through court dates, helping me investigate, and putting
in the time and work when I could not carry it all on my own.
Your strength and support made the impossible possible.

And finally, to every single mom who feels unseen,
unheard, or overwhelmed by life's battles—this book
is for you. Keep the faith. God is a God of miracles.
If He did it for me, He will do it for you too.

CONTENTS

INTRODUCTION

I am the third child of the family, the baby to Kay and Rudy Sea-mayer, and was born in Dallas, Texas. My parents were 20 and 30 years old when they got married. My Daddy was twenty-one years old when he came to America from Germany. My mom wrote his story, *The Last Train Out*, which is an incredible story of survival. The book is available on Amazon.

My sisters are Ann and Karen, who are two and seven years older than I am. My oldest sister Ann always reminds us that everything was great until we came along. Ha! Even though she says she's kidding, I think some of it is true.

We lived in Duncanville, Texas, throughout my childhood. My mom met her best friend, Mrs. Peggy, and Mrs. Shirley, and they have been family friends ever since.

My dad had a showroom at the World Trade Center with his own business. My mom helped too, but from home, while she was raising three kids.

We moved out to the country between Maypearl and Waxahachie when I was three years old. It was about 30 miles to downtown Dallas. My parents built their dream home, a 4,400 sq. ft, one-story, Bavarian-style home with two turrets. Many people said that it resembled a castle. We ate dinner at the table on the nights my dad was home. He traveled for work, so he was away on and off throughout the month. My mom was a fantastic cook, which is one of her many talents.

When I started kindergarten, I remember being so excited to ride the bus with my sisters. My mom would make us an egg sandwich, and we would walk down the long street to the little house my dad built for us to wait inside for the bus when it was cold or raining. We had so much fun riding our bikes everywhere and playing in the creek. We lived about five miles from our school. I remember riding my bike to school on field day. It was hot, and the road was gravel! I'll never forget the big hill that I went down, and no, I didn't fall! We would drink out of a water hose to quench our thirst! There were no such things as water bottles back then.

We were lucky enough to go on trips each summer to Galveston, which is where my mom grew up, and stay in a beach house. Crabbing and playing with cousins is what I remember, alongside riding the ferry and feeding the birds. We also went to Estes Park, Colorado, and stayed at the YMCA Camp of the Rockies. These memories have never left my mind. We had so much fun, having a weenie and marshmallow roast, riding on the go carts, and swimming in the indoor pool. I can still smell the chlorine. I also remember playing putt-putt golf and riding the Aerial Tramway to see the beautiful views, but as a child, all I was interested in was feeding the tiny little chipmunks. They would come right up to you for a peanut! We still have home movies of these memories.

But my favorite memory was hiking with my dad. My sisters and mom would go into town to shop, and he and I would point to a mountain and say, "Let's make it there today!" He would always find a stick and hand-carve a hiking stick, one for me and one for him. I collected bears of all types, both stuffed and little caricatures. I have always loved them, and I used to tell him that if we ran into a bear, I would just tell them that I was Erika and everything would be ok. I am thankful that we never ran into a grizzly!

Our Christmas was magical! Chucky, who was dad's best friend and the only grandfather we ever knew, was with us every Easter,

Thanksgiving, and Christmas. Aunt Pauline, who was a good friend of the family, also spent a lot of time with us. She was like a grandmother to me.

The gifts left out by Santa were like a movie set. I am grateful for all of these beautiful memories.

My parents divorced when I was nine years old, and we moved to an apartment in DeSoto, a town near where we lived before. Dad stayed at the big house. My mom went back to work, and you would think I would have been upset, but although I didn't like that they were divorced, it was fun living so close to friends, and we had a pool. We got to go on the weekends to see him, and since he traveled for work, it didn't seem much different than previous years.

Then we moved to some different apartments back in Duncanville where we had lived before. I was in the fifth grade, and on the first day of school, I heard some girls behind me whisper, "She's not in fifth grade!" I remember turning around and saying, "Yes, I am!" They were thinking that because I was tiny growing up. I wore a size 6X in the sixth grade, aware that it was the same size that most kindergarteners wore. Later, I became friends with those girls.

This is also where I met my boyfriend, who is now my husband of 14 years, Erik Williamson. We rode bikes together, and I taught him how to French kiss. I know, I know, don't judge me. The year before, when my parents got divorced, I was hanging out a lot with older kids my sisters' age, and someone was talking about it one day. So when I met Erik, I thought, I'll give it a try. Our friends thought it was cool, and they would say, "Hey Erik and Erika, y'all kiss." So we would.

My parents got back together just a year later, and we moved back to Duncanville to a house in Huntington Park, near Byrd Jr. High. I was now 11 years old, and by 12, I tried out for the tennis team and made it.

At 11 years old, my family discovered Cancun. Once we had the experience of the Caribbean, we never went back to Galveston. We would stay at all-inclusive resorts and have a blast! We also traveled to Jamaica, the Bahamas, and Germany for three weeks after picking up a brand new car in Frankfurt at the Mercedes factory. We drove all over Germany and met some of our relatives. Sigi and Detrich were our cousins. We had a blast as they showed us all around the "cool" places.

We moved to a bigger house in Duncanville for my high school years. We had a pool built, and both my parents were good with plants, so our yard always looked like a wedding venue.

I was into makeup and loved taking care of my skin. By now, I had also done my own school clothes shopping with my mom's credit card in hand. Looking back now I was spoiled, but with my parents success it gave them great pleasure in offering such a lifestyle. It was all I knew. My parents' business was going "gangbusters" (as my dad would say) in the 80s.

When I was 12, my parents bought me a Honda moped that I rode all over town, and I always had a friend in the back seat. Later, I found out that it was only made for one person. Oh, well.

My best friend and I used to make our own hair appointments in the sixth grade. We had so much fun getting a perm or a haircut and style from Carol! Good times.

My parents joined a brand new country club in Desoto. This is where I played tennis in addition to school. It was a blast, and I attended many tournaments with Coach Ken.

I cleaned houses of friends we knew and babysat from the time I was 11 years old. At 14, I lied and said I was 15 so I could work at Braum's Ice Cream Store. I was moved onto the food line, flipping burgers and having a great time, when one day the manager asked, "What year were you born?" I got caught, and they had to let me go. I loved working and had many jobs throughout my high school years.

Reflecting on my background, I realize how fortunate I was to grow up in an environment full of love, laughter, adventure, and perseverance. My childhood was full of wonderful things, from biking down gravel trails and gathering crabs on the beach to hiking mountains with Daddy or sneaking kisses with my future husband on the playground. Even during times of upheaval, such as my parents' divorce and frequent relocations, I always felt a sense of security in my family, friendships, and the values my parents instilled. These formative experiences have significantly affected who I am today—grateful, grounded, and keenly aware of both important and subtle moments that have fashioned my unique story. It may not have been ideal, but it was a wonderful journey that was completely mine.

PART I

LOVE, LABELS, AND THE LESSONS THAT SHAPED ME

CHAPTER ONE

THE EARLY YEARS: LABELED AND LOST

FINDING MY PLACE IN A WORLD THAT MISREAD ME

I have always been a carefree, happy-go-lucky kind of person. Some would even say silly, probably because of my childlike optimism. I have always seen the rainbow instead of the clouds in any situation, and in people as well.

At school, I was always laughing and in the "popular" group, or so I have been told. I genuinely connected with all kinds of people—those in the special needs class, the quiet and shy ones, the so-called 'outsiders', and everyone in between. It never mattered to me what group someone belonged to—I just valued people for who they were. I loved them all! That's probably how I ended up getting nominated for "Class Favorite" three years in a row in high school during the Valentine Coronation. There were over 900 kids in my class, and they voted for me! Coronation was an event where we would wear beautiful dresses and tuxedos, and we would pair up with somebody of our choice to walk through the "grand march." The student body would vote for different categories to award. Some of the categories included: Most Beautiful/Handsome; Duke/Duchess; and Class Favorite Boy/Girl. All three years, I walked with one of my best guy friends, Chris Martin—now known as *The Fashion Plate*—who has been living in Atlanta, Georgia, for years as an actor and entertainer.

Even though I was well-liked by my classmates, I felt labeled by some of the teachers as a troublemaker and rule breaker. I didn't get bullied by the students (as a lot of high school students go through). If I were bullied at all, it would have been by some of the principals and teachers. An educator's ability to recognize children's gifts and talents is so important in encouraging them to walk in their natural abilities. Unfortunately, this was not my experience. There were a handful of teachers who saw my heart and understood I was not trying to cause trouble or be disruptive. These teachers believed in me and helped me get through with my learning disabilities.

I'm an extreme extrovert. I get energy and fulfillment by being around other people, talking with them, helping them, and helping others succeed. I truly love it. But most of my teachers didn't see what I was trying to accomplish. They labeled me as talkative, a rule breaker, and a troublemaker. So, being well-liked by my friends and peers helped me to know that I was not a bad person and that helping others was a good thing.

A MASK OF LAUGHTER OVER SILENT STRUGGLES

Constantly being called out and getting in trouble during school due to educators' lack of understanding of my attention deficit disorder caused me to wear a mask to cover up the sorrow and sadness I felt inside. Sometimes I even felt like I was drowning in my depression. I wasn't depressed in general, but more towards school itself because of feeling misunderstood. Because of this, I never wanted others to feel the way I felt, and so I found great joy in finding ways to make other people laugh, feel joy, and be seen. I felt, and still do feel, that it is so important to be compassionate toward others and what they might be going through; to offer them grace and kindness even when we don't feel like it. We never know what burdens people are carrying.

I played tennis in both junior high and high school, largely influenced by both of my parents, who played and were active in many leagues. We lived close to the school and courts, so it was convenient to practice. In eighth grade, we joined a brand-new country club called Thorntree in Desoto, Texas, and I got to play in many tournaments through the club.

At Byrd Jr. High and Duncanville High School, I was on the traveling team, which was composed of the top six players. My best friend Becky was also on the traveling team, and together we had a blast competing with other schools. I believe we were able to get as good as we were because of attending Newk's Tennis Ranch and Newbrawnfuls early on in the 7th grade.

When I was a sophomore in high school, our coach of four years, Coach Walker, quit. He was a tough coach, but he was fun with his dry sense of humor, and we all loved him. We were all sad to see him go, but we were hopeful about the new coach. Unfortunately, he was not nice or fun at all—he never smiled. He had an intense and hardcore style of coaching that I didn't respond well to. Eventually, I quit. This would be a decision I would regret later on. I wish I would have talked with my parents as I think having that kind of influence and guidance would have been extremely helpful to make a better decision.

My parents were very loving, but to be honest, during this time of my life, they were busy with their careers and traveled quite a bit. I was the third child, and my older sisters had already moved out of the house, so I was on my own a lot. I was a fifteen-year-old trying to make very difficult decisions by myself. I felt overwhelmed without daily guidance. I didn't have a relationship with God at this time, either. I now know how having a relationship with Jesus would have helped me have the wisdom to make better decisions. But this is all a part of my story, and God is faithful all the time. So instead of wishing it were different, I suppose it is all a part of acceptance in understanding that God always has a plan. It is our attitudes that allow us to move forward even when we don't understand.

While in school, I also struggled with the traditional classroom style of teaching. I knew I was different, but I didn't understand why I couldn't learn like everyone else. My first memory of having any difficulty was in third grade. We were in reading class when we were doing SRA's (SRA Reading Laboratory), which is a personalized reading program that aids students in developing comprehension, vocabulary, and fluency skills through a color-coded, leveled system. Who remembers those? We would pick a story on a large card, like a file box with different subjects of stories, read the short story, and then answer about ten questions. As much as I enjoyed the stories, I realized that I couldn't answer the questions correctly. I just couldn't comprehend the facts to answer the questions. Later, I found out I was a visual, tactile learner. As a visual learner, you rely on what you see and benefit from illustrations and visual presentations. Visual learners generally like to take notes when learning and also doodle and draw while listening to a lecture.

Looking back, it makes perfect sense why I always loved big projects and creative assignments but struggled with the monotony of daily work. My brain was wired for color, story, and connection.

Through all of this, I found out I had an incredible memory, maybe because it was what I had to do for survival. The "art of cheating" became a survival tactic for me in order to pass classes. I spent several summers in school because of failing a class. I remember expressing my struggles with my mother and my teachers, and they ordered me to be tested with the school diagnostician. I will never forget them telling my parents that my IQ was normal and that I just was not trying. Interestingly enough, they had no idea about my productivity level of understanding, and that it had nothing to do with how high my IQ level was. The saddest part of it was that I truly was trying, but just couldn't comprehend their teaching styles, so therefore I fell through the cracks of public schools. I ended up getting put into special education classrooms, which, looking back, I feel was a travesty.

Do you remember having to take turns reading out loud in class? I do. When I was asked to read a paragraph, I would spend unnecessary time counting the paragraphs and people ahead of me so that I could practice reading my paragraph perfectly before it was my turn. Obviously, I wasn't hearing anything the other kids were reading before me. I literally thought that everyone else knew all of the words, meanings, and pronunciations, so if I came to a word that I couldn't read or pronounce, I would look dumb. So, what did I do? I would read the first few words, then begin to make up a fiction story of my own. This was a coping mechanism that I found worked pretty well. I figured that making people laugh and being the "class clown" was something I could do, even if I couldn't get all the words right. This way, everyone would just think that I was being funny, and it took the attention off the fact that I was a terrible reader. Even though this was not a conscious strategy at the time, looking back, it all makes sense.

I remember sitting in algebra class in Jr. High. After the teacher explained how to work the problems, I sat there without any understanding of how to do it. So, I raised my hand and asked if it would be ok if my friend sitting next to me could help me understand, as she always found a way to explain it to me, and the teacher said, "No." *Wow.* I remember sitting there for the rest of the class, 20 or 30 minutes, just doodling until the bell rang. *So sad!*

I had only one teacher in high school who cared enough to help me learn in a way that I could understand. Mrs. Barnes actually took the time to sit one-on-one and teach me. Even though I was disruptive to the class at times, she always found a way to offer her love and extra time to help me understand the assignment. Because of Mrs. Barnes, I finally felt understood, valued, and heard. We have remained friends throughout all of these years, and I am forever grateful for her love and care. It's amazing when just one person takes the time to help someone with their specific needs. Let this be a life lesson: that we all have understanding and knowledge of things that can absolutely change the course of someone's life if we pay attention.

Because of all of this and just being bored in school, I sincerely wanted to drop out in the tenth grade. I mean, I couldn't imagine quitting and not walking across the stage with all of my friends for graduation, but I just felt so isolated when it came to learning and getting any kind of help. I was consistently tardy for the first period and got in trouble for that, and even ended up in alternative school because I had exceeded the number of demerits allowed for being tardy, as was their protocol. *Seriously?* Most of the people in the alternative school were there because of more serious situations, such as possession of drugs, stealing, and other, more serious things. So, what was a girl from the nice part of town, with a loving family, known by most of her classmates as an optimistic, happy person, doing in an alternative school? You tell me! Years later, as I reflect on this time, I can't believe that not one person from my school—not a counselor, not a principal, not anyone—sat me down and asked, "Now listen, just what seems to be the problem?" *Not one!* I simply fell through the cracks of public school.

Being very ADHD led me to be a regular procrastinator and to try to fit too much into a small amount of time, usually by trying to meet someone else's needs. Which led me, ultimately, to being late for everything! I should never have been placed in an alternative school for a problem I was having with being tardy. For the record, I was supposed to be there for six weeks, but the day before I was released to go back to my high school with three weeks left of my junior year, my teacher/warden looked at me with a smile and said, "You aren't leaving here, we extended your time!" I had been celebrating my exit over lunch with a friend (by the way, this was the only time we were allowed to talk all day long). Can you even imagine how I must have felt? Abandoned, by everyone, with nobody to help me or to speak on my behalf. I also failed two classes because we were not allowed to go to our high school teachers for help on any assignment, because that was considered trespassing. There was no protocol for when one of the teachers would leave to take our work back to the high school. We never knew if he was just leaving to go to the bathroom or to take our work over to the high school. I always thought this was so crazy, and this is what led me to fail two classes. They even tried to extend my alternative school stint into my senior year, but thankfully, my reasonable and nice principal at Duncanville High School denied the request.

From sophomore year on, one of my best friends and I often drove to Booker T. Washington High School for the Performing and Visual Arts in downtown Dallas and picked up applications in hopes of attending a school that we could really thrive in, but our parents thought we were crazy for wanting to drive all that way, so we didn't ever apply. This was also a travesty. What could have been if I had been able to go to a school where I could express myself creatively instead of getting in trouble for my happy-go-lucky and positive personality!

My best advice to teachers and administrators is that when they have a student who has ADD/ADHD, or simply has different learning styles, is to simply give them a task. We love to help and oftentimes are just bored. This is why we end up disrupting the class or being the class clown. We can handle multitasking like you have never seen. Take a chance and ask what their interests are, and remember, it is not our intention to disrupt the class; we just need to be busy and need to feel valued.

Looking back, I often ponder how my life could have been different if I had attended Joe Blasco Makeup School and pursued my passion for special effects makeup, or if I had attended a school where I could express myself creatively instead of getting into trouble for my carefree personality. But then again, I wouldn't have had my beautiful daughter, Chelsea Laine.

GIFTS HIDDEN BENEATH THE LABELS

The same gift that made me want to help people in school—when I was always in trouble and not allowed to talk—was the same gift that led me to try to help Ben. I now know that helping others is one of my "gifts" and a significant part of my personality. Even though it drew me into a toxic relationship, it also shaped who I am today. From my earliest school days, through my struggles with learning styles, ADHD, and being misunderstood, to the passions I dreamed about and the relationships I chose, every piece has played a role in making me someone who sees people, values them, and wants to help them succeed.

DISCUSSION QUESTIONS

1. How did Erika's early labels impact her sense of identity?

2. What hidden gifts did Erika carry that were overlooked by authority figures?

3. In what ways have you felt misunderstood, and how did you cope?

Devotional Scripture: Psalm 139:14 — *I praise you because I am fearfully and wonderfully made.*

Reflection: God created you with intention. Even when others don't see your worth, God does.

Prayer: Lord, thank You for creating me with purpose. Help me to see myself through Your eyes, not the world's labels.

CHAPTER TWO

LOVE AND CODEPENDENCY

WHEN LOVE FEELS LIKE RESCUE

had been dating my boyfriend Ben since the summer after my ninth-grade year. Our relationship was never healthy. In my heart, I thought it was, or maybe just because he was my "first love," I made myself believe it was healthy. At age 17 (he was 18), I felt as if he were the love of my life, and the love we shared seemed real. We dated on and off for over three years, breaking up and reconciling over and over again. Every time we broke up, I felt as though my soul was being ripped apart.

At the time, I had not really been taught about waiting to have sex until I was married and all of the reasons why; I just felt it was morally right to wait to have sex until I was in a committed relationship and in love. Before I would "be with him," I told him that I wouldn't be "one of those girls" and waited until I thought he was truly committed. I had already heard of a few classmates who had to get abortions and knew I needed to protect myself from making that choice. So, I did what I thought was responsible and made my gynecology appointment to get on birth control.

Unfortunately, soon after we were together for the first time, I heard that he had been with another girl. Was it true? I'll never know for sure, but when I presented the information to him, he denied it. Being young and in love, I believed his story, and we stayed together.

On weekends, there were occasional house parties in our hometown, and many of them were hosted at my home because my parents traveled a lot and were out of town. The parties hosted at my house were very organized. (Ha!) We rolled up the oriental rugs, and our guests were told to sign into a guest book upon coming through the front door. I had a girlfriend who watched over the liquor cabinet so our friends wouldn't take advantage of my parents' things. She was tall, and although she was a sweet person, she also wouldn't take any crap from anyone. This helped me find comfort in making sure our parties did not get out of control. The streets were lined with cars, and the cops were only called a couple of times for noise or traffic. Most of the time, we had no problems; however, my boyfriend showed up many times drunk and under the influence of who knows what else. I was very naive to the fact that a lot of people were "on something" around me, other than alcohol.

One weekend at one of my parties, I heard someone say, "There is a fight outside," only to find out that it was my boyfriend, Ben. I was embarrassed, but really, constantly trying to help or fix him was a way of life for me. I was always rescuing him. Looking back now, I wish I had understood what was happening and how I was being codependent. There were times when we were alone and he was not under the influence of alcohol, when our relationship seemed good. It felt very much like love, or the love that I understood. The only problem was that he was a binge drinker, so that meant that he was basically a ticking time bomb in each and every corner of our lives.

Another time, he came over to my house after going to Dallas for the Texas/OU game, and he, of course, had been in yet another fight. After I refused to pick up his phone calls, he ended up outside my window, which was in front of our home in a circular driveway. He was pleading for me to come outside to see him, and when I wouldn't, he got angry, punched the window, and broke it. I was so scared of what my parents would think. Crazy stuff, right? I had to go and wake them, and my dad came out and drove him home.

Even though he paid to have the window fixed, that was the one time I truly remember wishing my parents, especially my dad, would have rescued me and forbidden me to see him. I was really strong-willed, and not sure I would have listened anyway, but I always felt that in my heart. And so, the chaotic cycle continued.

NIGHTS OF FEAR AND PLEADING

One night, his mom called to tell me that their family got into a big fight. He ultimately ran them out of the house with a gun in his hand and his anger running high—they all left as quickly as they could for their own safety to a neighbor's house. Why they didn't call the police, I'll never know, but after several hours of this, and him acting like Rambo in the trees and scaring everyone half to death, I guess he got tired and walked back into his house. I received a phone call around 1:00 a.m., and he proceeded to tell me that he was going to shoot himself. We stayed on the phone for a long time as I basically talked him out of killing himself, and he finally fell asleep. At age 17, I was having to act as a counselor, a rescuer, and a savior—not just a girlfriend. It was just a terrible situation. I remember putting my Bible next to me as I went to sleep and saying some prayers. I prayed a prayer that kind of went like this, "God, I am asking for your protection and to bring peace and calm to Ben. Just let him fall asleep."

I knew I couldn't do anything more about the situation. At last, I was relieved to hear his breathing change as he slid into slumber. I was finally able to take a deep breath and get some rest, knowing he was asleep and safe… For now.

The next day, I received a phone call from Ben. He said, "I'm calling to tell you goodbye." I said, "Where are you going? What do you mean by goodbye?"

He said, "My parents are taking me to rehab and I'll be gone for four to six weeks." Honestly, I can't really remember all of the conversation, but I do remember that I felt heartbroken. As crazy as it may sound, I was already missing him. A few weeks later, I went to visit Ben at the rehab facility. I will never forget the lady who worked there, probably a counselor or something, telling me that he was an alcoholic. I was so naive. I thought, *He's not an alcoholic! He just drinks too much.* I seriously thought the definition of an alcoholic was someone who was always drinking and whose hands shook. Ben didn't do that; he just would get drunk sometimes. I have come to know that I was not the only one who was lacking knowledge in this area of addiction. In my experience, later on in life, most people have very little knowledge about the addiction of alcoholism. Denial also plays a big part in this lack of understanding.

His parents asked me to keep this a secret, which was a terrible burden and caused a lot of stress that no teenager should have to face. I became very close with one of my guy friends, whom I confided in about Ben being in rehab, which helped me deal with the emotions that I had no business having to deal with at this age. He was in my English class and I had known him since the sixth grade. I trusted him, and he was a good listener, which I needed at the time. Looking back now, I'll bet he thought I was crazy to not just break up with Ben and move on with my life.

TRAPPED BY A TIE I COULDN'T SEE

The question is, how or why did I stay with him time and time again? After the drunken fights, apologizing, I forgave him and believed all of the lies that he would never do it again. All of these years later, it raises the question. *Why?* It would be years later that I would encounter a lot of spiritual and personal growth while attending our home church and going through a program called the *Road Adventure.*[1]

The Road Adventure encourages, equips, and empowers people to live life to the fullest. It provides the tools needed to overcome the emotional damage that may have been from your past or present, as well as face future challenges in life.

I also attended another retreat years later called *Heart Quest at Fellowship of the Sword,* which helps to uncover truth, unlock identity, and unleash the passion and purpose within you.[2]

These studies brought up the question for me: could it have been something else? How would my life have gone if I had not been trapped in a toxic relationship? If I had not chosen to have sex at 17 for the first time, which blurred my vision of right and wrong, how would my subsequent years have unfolded?

Were my choices a result of generational sin and impact, or a pattern I had learned from my childhood years? Or, simply, was this just my story on its own? Now looking back, I believe it was a mix of all of those things. I'm not sure what makes some people accept this kind of behavior in a relationship, while others can simply walk away.

Through years of seeking to heal, I learned that these types of behaviors were key markers of an unhealthy, codependent relationship. When I first heard the word codependent, I had no idea what it meant. Codependency *"confuses caretaking and sacrifice with loyalty and love."* Characterized by excessive emotional or psychological reliance on a partner, typically one who requires support on account of an illness or addiction.[3] In my case, this looked like caring for someone who was a binge drinker, drug user, and bipolar.

I didn't understand that I was held captive, stuck in a stronghold called a *soul tie*, that would not let me walk away from this destructive situation. There are healthy soul ties, such as those between a new mother and her baby or between a husband and a wife. However, an unhealthy soul tie is a destructive relationship that feels like a force you can't walk away from, even though you know you should.

It was years until I learned the fullness of the definition of codependency and truly understood why I had struggled and felt trapped for so long. Even after walking through a lot of healing, it was many more years before I was free from this pattern, which was an unhealthy cycle.

At this time in my life, I prayed at night and whenever I needed help. I did believe in God, but I did not have an understanding of a personal relationship with Jesus. That would come later.

DISCUSSION QUESTIONS

1. What early signs of codependency can you identify in Erika's relationship with Ben?

2. Why do you think Erika stayed, even when she was hurt?

3. How do we sometimes confuse love with responsibility?

Devotional Scripture: Galatians 1:10 — *Am I now trying to win the approval of human beings, or of God?*

Reflection: When we seek to fix others to feel loved, we often lose sight of God's love for us.

Prayer: God, help me to seek Your approval above all. Teach me how to love without losing myself.

CHAPTER THREE

THE PROPOSAL THAT CHANGED EVERYTHING

TRADING CLASSROOMS FOR REAL LIFE

After all of the discouragement in high school and feeling defeated with the education system, I never thought college would be an option for me. To be honest, the thought never crossed my mind. We never talked about it at home, which was a little weird to me because later I learned that my dad had graduated from college in Germany with a horticulture degree. My mom went to college and was offered two scholarships, one for music and one for basketball. When some of my friends were planning on going up to our high school to take the SAT test, I remember saying, "I'm not coming to school on a Saturday to take a test!" I know it sounds strange, but I had no idea what it was even about. All I wanted to do was get out of school as soon as possible because it felt more like a jail to me. As a side note, I loved learning, not just sitting at a desk.

I opted to participate in a work release for school, which suited me. I left after the fourth period and went to work at a daycare center in the infant room. I always loved babies, so it was fun, and I didn't have to be at school, where I felt as if I was wasting my time. In my senior year, I went through a strenuous course to learn life-saving techniques, including CPR, and then taught swimming classes at a daycare for 2 to 5-year-olds. It was one of the hardest trainings I had ever been through, but it was worth it, and I was proud of myself for completing it.

STANDING OUT IN MY OWN WAY

As the evening of our senior prom approached, most of my friends shopped at Terry Costa in Dallas for their dresses. I had done it in the past for other occasions, but this time, I talked my mom into letting me have my dress custom-made. I designed it to be totally unique and different, which fits my personality perfectly. It was a beautiful mermaid-fit jade green material with a row of rhinestones below my knees, followed by pink lace in a two-foot-long train. I was into the fashions of Prince, Madonna, Cindy Lauper, and Boy George. It was glamorous, to say the least.

Graduation was coming up, and since I had been chosen for class favorite and was known as a funny person, I was trying to think of something that I could do that would be funny but wouldn't get me in trouble. One day, I stopped at a garage sale and noticed a pair of platform shoes. They were totally out of style at the time, completely hilarious, and perfect for my plan. I remember telling my friend, "This is it. I will wear these shoes to walk across the stage, and it will be my final funny moment at DHS."

As we were in preparation, lining up for the big moment at grad-uation, a teacher saw me change shoes and said, "Erika, you don't want to do that, you will embarrass your parents!" I replied, "My mom already knows." I am glad I did not listen to a closed-minded, boring teacher and instead followed my heart and my gut instinct. I walked across the stage, stopped in the middle, lifted my gown a little so that everyone could see my shoes, and then turned my shoes outward to show them off, and just like I had planned, everyone laughed. Not only did they laugh, but I also got a standing ovation. Making people laugh gave me a good feeling of belonging and happiness. After I walked off the stage, you're not even going to believe who came up to me and hugged me with a big smile—that teacher who told me not to do it! Let this be a lesson: don't ever let anyone's personal insecurities stop you from being you, because if you do, you might end up missing opportunities that God has for you!

After graduation, we had a little get-together at our house with some of our family friends before I was off to the senior parties.

Following high school, I enrolled at a beauty school and earned my esthetician license and then a nail technician license. I was pretty comfortable with this type of work already, as my sister was a nail artist and had already started teaching me how to do sculptured nails.

At this point, I was 19 years old, and Ben and I had been broken up for ten months before we started talking again. It's funny how you can desperately miss someone and only remember the good times and somehow forget all of the bad. This is a good example of an unhealthy soul tie, which can be very dangerous. Looking back, I didn't have a relationship with God as I do today. I should have sought out counseling before getting back with Ben instead of relying on my own emotions. But, at this point in time, I simply had no direction for my life.

SAYING YES FOR ALL THE WRONG REASONS

Ben enlisted in the Army in 1989 and was stationed at Ft. Sill in Oklahoma. There was no internet, texting, or even cell phones, so we relied on occasional expensive long-distance phone calls and many, many handwritten letters. One day, I received a letter that said he might be stationed in Germany. He wrote in his letter, *We can get married if you want to.* I was bored with my life and thought, *What else do I have to do?* How exciting the thought of moving to Germany! So, young and blind, I accepted. Funny how our hearts grow softer over time, but little did I know that he hadn't changed at all. I thought he needed me, and since no one else needed me at that time, maybe I could help him. I was depending on my own understanding rather than asking and praying to God for HIS counsel and guidance.

On one of his visits to see me before we were married, he ended up with a DUI and had to spend some time in jail. His license was revoked, and I had to drive him back and forth to work. Why couldn't I see the truth? After we were married, he had to serve extra time on weekends to pay off the debt he owed his attorney.

My mom said later that she and my sisters tried to talk me out of getting married. To be honest, I don't remember having a sit-down, serious conversation about it. Nobody tried to paint a picture of how my life would be if I married Ben. I only remember arguments and quick discussions about it, but nothing more. I am not blaming my family. I just don't remember getting true advice or guidance.

It is far more profitable to look to God for wisdom in a Biblical perspective to teach and train your children than it is to rely on human understanding. I wasn't raised that way, so it makes sense that my parents didn't guide me Biblically. But now I know just how important it is to be in a good Bible-based church with supportive friends.

DISCUSSION QUESTIONS

1. Why do you think Erika accepted Ben's proposal despite the red flags?

2. How can feelings of purposelessness influence our decisions?

3. Have you ever pursued a change in circumstances, hoping it would fix deeper issues?

Devotional Scripture: Proverbs 3:5-6 — *Trust in the Lord with all your heart and lean not on your own understanding.*

Reflection: Change doesn't always bring clarity. When we lean on God, not circumstances, we find lasting direction.

Prayer: Father, help me trust You with my future. Give me wisdom to recognize the difference between Your plans and my own desires.

CHAPTER FOUR

A WAR AT HOME

A WEDDING AND A SHATTERED DREAM

Ben and I married on October 14, 1989. We had a beautiful wedding and honeymoon. What should have been a wonderful life was destroyed by his constant bad decisions. I felt like my life was on hold and topsy-turvy at all times due to the instability. Because of his DUI arrest, we were stripped of the opportunity of being stationed in Germany, which was very disappointing to me. My dad was from Germany, and I had been so excited at the thought of living in the country of my heritage. This was another dream shattered in my life.

After ten months of marriage, Ben received orders to go to Desert Shield, which was the prelude to the war that turned into Desert Storm. Since I had no idea how long he would be gone, I moved back to my hometown in Texas to live with my parents while he was gone.

We wrote letters almost every day while he was gone. This was a very difficult time for me at 21 years old. The thought never left my mind that, at any time, I could receive the knock at the door that

Ben had been killed in war. While I was waiting for Ben, I kept busy working on temporary jobs. One of my favorites was at the salon at Stanley Korshak in the Crescent Hotel in downtown Dallas. I was working with a good friend of mine as a receptionist. She was a hair stylist and we had worked together before at the Verandah at the Anatole Hotel in Dallas. We had a great time together!

LAUGHTER IN THE WAITING

It was during this season of life that I met Granny Anderson. She was the mother of one of my sister's friends. She was in her 70s and the epitome of a sweet grandma. God knew I needed her in my life! Because I didn't have living grandparents, as mine all passed away before I was born or when I was very young, I loved being around older people with their wisdom, advice, and stories. There were a few that I adopted as "my own" grandparents, and Granny Anderson was one of these special people.

Her son, Radar, and his wife, Lucy, had a booth at the State Fair of Texas and invited me to come work with them. We did temporary tattoos together and had a blast! She and I got really close that summer. I needed to laugh during this sad time, and boy, did she offer the laughs! It was so good to have joy back in my life.

I would go over to Granny's house to visit or just help her with household tasks. Occasionally, I would drive her to a doctor's appointment. As we were leaving one of the doctor's appointments, she noticed some beautiful purple cabbage that was a part of the landscape. I was talking to her and then noticed she had fallen behind. I turned around, and she was on her knees, about to dig up the beautiful purple cabbage. She said, "That is a damn waste!" I had to talk her into not digging it up, then I laughed out loud as she kept murmuring under her breath about how she thought it was such a waste.

Granny used to tell me stories of how she had stood up for herself in different instances when something was wrong. She would say, "I have a hell of a right and a better left!" She only weighed about 100 pounds, but she was feisty! I loved hearing all of her stories. Eventually, dementia set in, and her mind went. But bless her heart, she was such a highlight in my life!

One afternoon while Ben was still deployed, I was running errands. I had gone to get an oil change at the local business right behind my parents' house. Erik was the manager at their family business, and he and I had gone to school together since elementary school. In the fifth grade, we were "boyfriend/girlfriend" until he broke up with me at the pencil sharpener one day. Imagine my surprise when I saw him at the Oil X Change shop. We started chatting, and I found out that he was married and already had a child. We had a great time catching up! I drove away thinking, "He is such a nice guy!" However, later I found out that a friend who worked there saw us interacting and said, "Those two will end up together."

Ben was gone for over seven months when I finally received word that he would be coming back to the States in approximately a week. So, I decided to pack up my car and drive back to Oklahoma to be there to greet him upon his return. I stayed with Nonie, who was also a military wife, so we could await our spouses' arrival. Since I was going a few days early, I thought it would be a good idea to look for a job, which ended up being easier than I thought. At the time, I was a nail technician, so I usually had my nails painted in some unique way. I walked into a tanning salon simply to get myself an appointment, and a lady saw my nails that I had painted with an American flag on one nail and a Texas flag on another, and went wild. She asked me, "Did you hand-paint those?" I told her that I had. I didn't think much of it as it was easy for me. She told me that her sister was looking for a nail technician and to call her. She asked me to meet with her the next day at six in the morning. *In the morning!*

I was 21 years old and thought, *I want a job, but not that bad!* I managed to set up the interview for the evening instead. I had taken a nap and overslept, so I jumped up to rush to the salon for my interview. When I drove up, it was already dark, and the owner, Donna, thought I was there for a tanning appointment and was going to tell me that I would have to reschedule.

After a long day, she apparently had forgotten about my interview. I went in with great confidence and said, "I'm Erika. I'm here for the interview and I do sculptured nails! Not tips." I was really proud of my skill. It was so funny. Regardless of my blunder, I was hired! We became fast friends, despite our different definitions of "morning." She would arrive for work at five in the morning, and I wouldn't roll in until ten o'clock. I would be asking, "What's for breakfast?" and she would be saying, "When's lunch?" She is one of my best friends to this day! I loved my job with Donna at Clippers Inn! We ran a two-for-one special in the paper and advertised nails by "Erika from Dallas." I was booked with a full clientele in just a few months. God's favor was on my life!

THE WAR COMES HOME

The day Ben came home was a day I'll never forget. I was newly married, and my husband was coming home safely after seven months at war. I was happy to see him. It was almost euphoric! But unfortunately, the happiness that I felt didn't last long. Ben had seen a lot of terrible things while fighting for our country and was probably suffering from PTSD. Between his family issues growing up and past drinking problems, this only made his issues of anger and addiction worse.

Following Ben's return from Desert Storm, I endured a lot of emotional abuse as his drinking continued to spiral out of control. I was trapped in a nightmare of erratic, nonsensical fights, far-fetched accusations, and late-night returns without transparency about where he had been. He was upset about $700 I couldn't account for while he was gone for 7 months. Then one day, out of the blue, he accused me of getting an abortion. (For the record, I was not pregnant.) I was devastated by his behavior. We continued to live in Oklahoma for another year until he finished his assignment.

DISCUSSION QUESTIONS

1. How did Granny Anderson's presence offer Erika a different kind of support?

2. What small joys helped Erika hold on to hope during Ben's deployment?

3. Who in your life has been an unexpected source of peace?

Devotional Scripture: Isaiah 26:3 — *You will keep in perfect peace those whose minds are steadfast, because they trust in you.*

Reflection: Even in uncertain times, God sends peace through people, moments, and His Word.

Prayer: God, thank You for the people who quietly remind me that peace is still possible. Help me to notice Your presence every day.

PART II

CAUGHT IN
THE STORM

CHAPTER FIVE

BACK TO TEXAS, BACK TO TROUBLE

LIVING WITH DR. JEKYLL AND MR. HYDE

Following Ben's assignment in Oklahoma, we moved back to Texas because that's where our families lived. We got an apartment in a city close to our hometown. We were both working, and he decided to go to college since the military would pay for it.

We were trying to get settled back into our marriage and life together, but he was drinking a lot and often was drunk. When Ben was sober, everything was fine. We got along and had some good memories. But then he would drink too much and turn into a completely different person. You may remember the Dr. Jekyll and Mr. Hyde story? I felt like I was living that nightmare. Ben's drunken spurts always led to a disastrous evening of fighting. Sometimes we would go out for a day at the lake, and he would drink too much, and the yelling and screaming would continue. I would try to stop it before it started by saying, "Haven't you had enough?" or "Aren't we having enough fun?" I didn't realize that was actually the worst thing I could have done, but at the time, I didn't know any better. I would try to convince him that enough is enough to prevent the fights. To make matters worse, Ben had a habit of getting his guns out while he was drunk so he "could clean them."

Looking back, because of his behavior, I am sure he had some level of post-traumatic stress disorder. As crazy as it all sounds, I got used to hiding his guns from him when he would be drinking. I look back and think that was completely insane! I didn't even realize this was a life-threatening situation for me.

ROCKS, GUNS, AND THE NIGHT I WENT NUMB

One evening as we were driving back from a party, I remember having fun and thinking, "We didn't even get into a fight!" This would turn out to be another nightmare of an evening together. After a messed-up order at a fast-food drive-through, he irrationally exploded. It wasn't even his burger. It was mine. I told him it was no big deal, but his anger elevated. He yelled at me to go back and for them to fix it. I convinced him it was ok and we started back home. As we began to turn to get back on the highway, he said, "Let me out!"

I was confused. "What?" "Why?" He grabbed the steering wheel, so I had no choice but to pull over and let him out of the car. I rolled down the window and begged him to get back into the car, as it was probably 1 a.m. He refused. I was at the bottom of the hill on the service road, and he had run up to the highway. He began to throw rocks down at my car! I decided to roll up my window and drive home. In all of this craziness, I thought he could have hit me in the head with one of those rocks. He began running along the highway, and I even tried one more time to get him to get into the car, but he just ignored me. I thought to myself, *Listen, dummy, just leave him and drive back home!* So, I did. When I got home, I got ready for bed and, as usual, hid his guns.

This had started to be a regular routine for us, and I didn't even realize how crazy it was that I stayed. He would get drunk and then decide to clean his guns (or whatever it was he was doing with them). When he got back home about 45 minutes later, he asked right away, "Where are my guns?" I wouldn't tell him, which sparked yet another argument. He wouldn't give up, so I eventually showed him where I had hidden his guns and then went back to bed. I had no idea what he was doing. At this time, I was just numb. Can you believe that I was just lying in bed trying to go to sleep? Looking back now, I realize how dangerous this all was. In my desperation to help him and keep our marriage, I put up with all of this, thinking it would somehow get better.

One night around that time, I remember Ben's brother was going through a rough time, so we were going to take him out to dinner and hang out with him that evening. For no good reason, as was his regular routine, Ben started a huge fight with me. I, of course, was crying, confused, furious, and felt very defeated at this point. Before I knew it, they left to go out without me. In hindsight, that was probably his plan all along! As the night went on, I watched the clock pass midnight and then one o'clock before I decided to just go to sleep. When I awakened around six that morning and they were still not home, I was livid! We didn't have cell phones back then, but Ben and I did have pagers. Finally, around 7:00 AM, they walked in the door. I was furious and demanded to know where they had been. They were still drunk and high on drugs. His brother started to call me names and then came at me physically. Ben had to step in and hold him back!

This was the last straw; I had dealt with this sort of erratic behavior for the last time. We told our family that we were getting a divorce. I was very calm about it. I was just *done!* I knew I had to do something drastic.

BETRAYAL WRAPPED IN A BLESSING

During the past year, I had gotten off birth control, and we had been using the rhythm method for birth control. Although the fights escalated and my fear of the future arose, we were trying to be cordial about the breakup. Maybe it was part of our goodbye, but he convinced me to be intimate one more time.

The scary thing is that when someone has an addiction, they are desperate. There is no doubt in my mind that Ben did what he did on purpose. He used the possibility of pregnancy as a form of entrapment and manipulation, so I would have to be in his life forever due to our shared child. Out of this betrayal came a blessing, our daughter.

DISCUSSION QUESTIONS

1. What signs did Erika notice that showed the situation was becoming more dangerous?

2. What does it take for someone to recognize their "last straw" moment, and how might that decision change the course of their life?

3. What does hope look like during chaos for you?

Devotional Scripture: Romans 5:3-5 — *Not only so, but we also glory in our sufferings, because we know that suffering produces perseverance; perseverance, character; and character, hope.*

Reflection: Even in chaos, God is shaping us for something greater. Hope is forged in the fires we survive.

Prayer: Lord, when life feels like too much, help me remember You are forming hope in me through every trial.

CHAPTER SIX

FAITH AWAKENS

THE DAY TWO LINES CHANGED EVERYTHING

I proceeded to move out of the apartment and move in with one of my best friends. It was about three weeks later that I was at a friend's graduation ceremony, and we were going to stop and get something to eat, but nothing sounded good. I didn't think much of it.

When I missed my period, I began to wonder if I might be pregnant, so I decided to take a home pregnancy test. The test read positive. I was home alone. I was crying, thinking, *I was done with him!* Holding my tummy, the thought crossed my mind once, and only once, that maybe, *just maybe*, I could have an abortion. Then I started crying harder, apologizing to the baby and to God for the thought ever crossing my mind. I felt hopeless. I had dealt with so much craziness with Ben through the years. I didn't want the nightmare to continue, raising a baby with someone who had such an addiction problem. I called my mom and, through my tears, I said, "Can you come over?"

I guess it was motherly intuition. She said, "You're pregnant, aren't you?" Crying, I told her I was, and we continued talking until I calmed down.

I remember talking to Ben on the phone (knowing I was pregnant) but not telling him. I was just fishing around to see what he would say. I asked him, "What if I were?"

He said, "Are you?" I didn't answer him. I just said goodbye and hung up the phone. I needed time to think about how I would tell him and what I was going to do. Would we raise this child alone, or together? To be honest, I really had no idea what it all would look like.

After a couple of weeks, we decided to get back together and have this baby. He had agreed to stop drinking. (Little did I know that there was a BIG BEAR sleeping inside of him.) We decided to go over to each of our parents' houses and tell them over dinner that we had decided to stay together and that I was pregnant.

My parents were supportive and happy to have their first grandchild. Telling his mom and stepdad was another story. They knew we loved each other very much, even through all of the issues. All they kept saying was, "Well, you know, y'all were separated!" I couldn't imagine why they kept saying that. I was completely naive about what they were trying to get me to read between the lines. When I realized what they were saying, I was appalled. What they were saying was, *Y'all were separated, and the baby might not be Ben's!* To be honest, I could only wish that it wasn't his, but I had gotten pregnant before I had even left. I would have to be an idiot to say, *Hey, I'm pregnant!* And then get back with someone I was divorcing. How stupid.

WHAT? I was furious! Who did they think I was? I had gotten pregnant before I had even moved out; I just didn't know it. But I shouldn't have been surprised. They had always been hateful to me behind my back and sarcastic to my face. It wasn't a comfortable relationship. This should have been another sign to get out of the relationship. This was another terrible stress factor for me.

A CALM BEFORE THE STORM

During my pregnancy, things were great. We rented an adorable house on the edge of Ft. Worth, close to Arlington. Ben was working at his uncle's law firm and was going to school full-time. He had plans to go to law school. He wasn't drinking, and we had a calm home for the moment.

When you have a relationship with an addict, things are good as long as they are not under the influence of the substance. When they are drunk or high, it is a nightmare. Up and down, fighting and making up, *all the time...* is exhausting. I would always say, "He is so sweet!" but then would make excuses for him when he would drink too much and fight. That's what you do when you are in love with someone with this disease.

I knew in my heart that so much of our relationship was not normal, inconsistent to say the least, but I didn't know how to make it right or change it. Now, all of these years later, I know that you *cannot change anyone*; they have to want it for themselves, and in all my experiences, the only time they ever truly come clean with drugs or alcohol is by having a God-encounter. *God is a God of miracles!* Programs like Alcoholics Anonymous and Celebrate Recovery are wonderful and offer great support; however, without a relationship with God, most people eventually fall back into addiction. John 8:12, *Jesus says, "I am the light of the world. Whoever follows me will never walk in darkness, but will have the light of life"* (NIV).

MY FIRST STEPS TOWARD FAITH

While Ben was working, I got a job as a nail technician at a really nice salon called Hair Logics. It was owned by a wonderful Christian lady named Darlene. When I was interviewing, I thought she wouldn't hire me because I was pregnant. She told me, "This is a Christian salon. We play Christian music, we have Bible Studies, and we pray for one another."

I was a believer, but had not been around people like her. I was not going to church at the time, except for some holidays. I was not used to being in a Christian environment. Darlene hired me as a nail tech and became one of my best friends and a mentor to me, and still is to this day, 30 years later.

I loved the girls I worked with and felt a lot of peace there at the salon. I noticed many differences in the women I worked with. They were very kind and loving. One of my favorite things that we did was pray before our monthly meetings. Before working at Hair Logics, my prayers were mostly the old rhyme, "Now I lay me down to sleep, I pray to the Lord my soul to keep, If I should die before I wake, I pray to the Lord my soul to take!" Then I would pray for my family and go to bed.

But at Darlene's salon, we would start each meeting with a question: "Does anyone have anything they want us to pray for?" This was my first *real* experience in living the Christian lifestyle.

Most of the girls at the salon went to a non-denominational, Bible church. I had never experienced anything like it before. The Christian music that Darlene played in the salon really affected me. I was feeling deep emotions when I heard it. I felt moved, happy, joyful, and tearful at times. Now I know it was the Holy Spirit moving in my heart.

Ben and I started attending Darlene's church. The messages the pastor was preaching were so different from anything I had ever experienced. I actually could understand the sermons in a way that I could apply them to my life. Never before had I experienced this. I really liked it and wanted more of it. I started going to church regularly, and Ben came with me most of the time. It was the change I needed, and looking back, I am so grateful. Choosing to attend church had changed the course of my life forever. The Bible says we are not meant to do life alone. Community is so important, and attending church regularly, even volunteering, will take you to deeper level of your faith.

I have to say that my real spiritual journey began while I was working with Darlene at Hair Logics. It was also during this time that one of my clients, Beth Ann, invited me to work with her at Mary Kay Cosmetics. Mary Kay's philosophy was: God first, family second, and career third. These concepts changed my life.

DISCUSSION QUESTIONS

1. What made Erika's encounter with faith during pregnancy so impactful?

2. How did the community help shift her understanding of God?

3. What does it mean for you to encounter Jesus personally?

Devotional Scripture: Jeremiah 29:13 — *You will seek me and find me when you seek me with all your heart.*

Reflection: True transformation begins when we open our hearts to God's presence, especially in seasons of vulnerability.

Prayer: Jesus, thank You for meeting me in the quiet and unexpected places. Draw me near to Your heart.

CHAPTER SEVEN

CHAOS ERUPTS

PROOF ON TAPE

Life continued, and I was about four months pregnant now. At this point, Ben and I had been together for six years and had been married for four years. The thought of having a baby and starting our family was concerning to me. While I am very close to my family, Ben has never been close to his. Even though Ben's family acted civil in my presence, there was always sarcasm and an atmosphere of hostility. I had heard many rumors about my family and me personally that had stemmed from remarks from his family. This upset me and made me very uncomfortable, but since I didn't have proof, I just let it slide.

One day after we moved into our house, we were having a refrigerator delivered. We were both busy working, so we asked Ben's mother to come to the house and wait for the delivery for us. She agreed and came over. When I got home, she was gone, and I went to listen to the messages on the answering machine. Remember those days? I noticed the message light was on longer than usual. I thought,

Gosh, how many messages did I get today? So, I hit the button and began to listen to the messages. Apparently, when Ben's mother was there waiting for the delivery guy, she picked up a call on our phone. It was Ben's grandmother. The machine recorded their entire 20-minute conversation. I couldn't believe what I was hearing. There it was. Right in front of me. The proof that Ben's mother and stepfather couldn't stand me or my family. The conversation was full of hate, accusations, and mockery. Here was the proof of what I had always believed to be true, but was unsure. My eyes filled with tears of hurt as the emotion of anger set in. The answering machine had recorded the entire phone conversation and caught them on tape (literally). They were always so fake to our faces, and this was recorded proof. I was understandably shaken, hurt, and felt so sad about the situation.

Needless to say, being pregnant, tired, and hormonal, I refused to deal with this kind of drama and stress alone. So, I called Ben at work and told him what happened. He called his mom and let her know that she had been recorded and that I had heard everything they were saying. Knowing that she knew I heard how hateful they had been to me, I had hoped that she would call me and apologize. I kept waiting for her to call me and apologize. After all, she's Ben's mother! She's the parent! I waited for about three weeks, and that call never came. I was so stressed, angry, and frustrated—but mainly hurt. So, I decided to call her and address the situation. I did not want to go to the next family function and act like nothing happened, even though their normal way of dealing with issues is to ignore the obvious.

As I picked up the phone to call her, I felt my heart was going to beat out of my chest. I was so nervous. The conversation didn't go well at all. It ended with her screaming and hanging up on me, which she later lied to her son that I hung up on her. That was simply not true. After that, all I knew was that they were out of our lives now, at least for a little while. During this time, I was learning a lot from my coworkers and the church we were attending as I grew in my relationship with Jesus. I was definitely seeking more peace in my life. I had lived with such chaos, and it felt wonderful to experience some levels of peace and joy. I also learned about setting boundaries with my relationships and toxic situations, even if it included my own family.

JOY IN THE MIDDLE OF THE STORM

On January 12, 1994, I gave birth to the most precious little baby girl, Chelsea Laine. I truly experienced joy like never before. As happy as I was, my heart was hurting that our families could not be together and celebrate this momentous occasion. Ben and I still had not heard from his family since the recorded conversation incident and the terrible call with his mother. We just didn't feel comfortable inviting them to the hospital. We wanted to avoid any drama or awkwardness. I know that is so sad, but it's just where we were emotionally. We did, however, invite my family and several friends when I went into labor. After a very long and tough labor, our sweet baby girl had arrived. She was 7 pounds on the dot and 19 ¾ inches long. It was an awesome celebration!

Since we lived about 45 minutes away from the hospital, we went to my parents' house, which was close by, the night after Chelsea Laine was born. Staying with them made it possible for friends and family to visit our new little bundle. I had not had much of an appetite throughout my pregnancy. So when we arrived, my mom had made an amazing home-cooked meal. It was beautiful and I was starving! It was such a wonderful welcome for our little family.

The next day, we went back to our home in Ft. Worth. I loved our little house. It was on a beautiful lot with many trees and beautiful windows. I felt very happy. Having a new baby in the house was such a joy. I had been babysitting infants since I was ten years old.

Being with children was very natural for me, and I loved being a mommy.

After two weeks, I went back to work at the salon. I desperately wanted to be home with my sweet baby, so I crammed a five-day work week into two. My mom and dad kept Chelsea Laine on Tuesdays, and Ben kept her on Saturday. It was so hard to be away from her, but I was thankful to have them care for her.

In addition to working at the wonderful salon, I was also selling Mary Kay Cosmetics. I loved the freedom of setting my own hours and working with my clients. Teaching skin care and makeup was fun for me. My sister Karen came over once a week to help me with the house and babysit. While she was there at the house, I could work on my side job. Ben was still working and going to school full-time. In the afternoons, he would come home. Many times I would have dinner made, and Chelsea Laine and I would be playing in the front yard waiting for his arrival. Ben and I also continued to attend church. We had Chelsea Laine dedicated when she was about five months old. We were having a very happy life. I felt as if things were just right but unfortunately, things took a turn just as they always had in the past.

A DOOR I SHOULDN'T HAVE OPENED

We still had not spoken to Ben's parents. One day, I was thinking about it and feeling bad that our baby was seven months old and had not met her other grandparents. I tried to put our differences aside and arranged a meeting. As much as I felt that I was doing the right thing, I made the decision on my own without praying and asking God what His thoughts were. When you pray and ask the Lord for His direction, He will guide you through thoughts or ideas, and you will feel peace to make the right decision. I would later regret this decision of not praying first.

The visit went as well as you would expect under the past turmoil. I was not comfortable having them in our home at all, but I thought it was the right thing to do. That's when I learned that I cannot control things and fix everything on my own. It's best to pray about everything and leave things up to God and wait for *HIS* direction and steps to take.

THE BABY SHOWER AND THE SWAT TEAM

Chelsea Laine and I went to a baby shower in our hometown, about 45 minutes away. She was about seven months old. We got back a little earlier than I had expected. As I drove up our long driveway, I noticed Ben's car parked out front with the door open. It was a beautiful day out. I was excited that we had gotten home early so we could spend some family time together. Our schedules were so busy, so an afternoon together would be a treat.

He must've stopped by the house to pick something up, and apparently was leaving. When he came out of the front door, I said hello and asked him where he was going. He had on his soccer clothes and said he was headed to the park to kick the soccer ball around. I said, "Oh, ok! Wait just a minute, and I will get a blanket, and Chelsea Laine and I will come and join you." All of a sudden, he became angry. He began to say things like, "I never get to do anything by myself!" This was simply not true. We began arguing, and he got in his car and left. I was instantly mad, and my blood was boiling. I got in my car and started to follow him around the neighborhood. How crazy was this? I had a seven-month-old baby in the back of my car and started thinking, *Who does this sort of thing?* So, after driving around too fast in our neighborhood trying to chase him down, I decided, even as mad as I was, how ridiculous the whole thing was, so I just drove home. This was around four o'clock on a

Sunday afternoon. Of course, I was upset, mad, and confused, but I had to go into mom mode. I was good at switching from sad to happy at a moment's notice.

I did not hear from him all afternoon or evening. I went ahead and did my normal evening routine of feeding Chelsea Laine, eating dinner by myself, and getting ready for bed. Sometime around ten o'clock that night, he came rolling in. I was in my bed watching TV, and Chelsea Laine was in her crib in the next room, asleep. He came into the bedroom where I was lying down, and lay next to me, then proceeded to grab the remote control and change the channel, which of course made me mad. He was a master at picking fights.

I said to him, "Listen, if you want to watch something other than what I'm watching, please go into the living room. I was here first, and this is what I'm watching." He looked over at me with evil in his eyes, and for the first time, I truly felt scared of him. I realized that he was wasted. I'm not sure what—alcohol or some sort of drugs—I didn't know, but he looked crazy.

He got up and left the room, and I remember hearing a voice plain as day telling me, *Get up and get out!* So, I did just that. I got up out of bed and I tried to stay as calm as possible. I started packing my clothes and my things, walking from my bedroom to the bathroom. When I walked back into our bedroom, his sawed-off shotgun was leaning against our dresser. Of course—as usual—living in this crazy situation, I took the gun and hid it under the bed. He came back into the room and said, "Where is my gun?" I ignored him for as long as I could, but he eventually found it. Chelsea Laine was still sleeping in her room. I heard him say something under his breath about me not taking Chelsea Laine away from the house. When I heard that, it scared me, as I couldn't imagine what was to come next. I was talking as calmly as possible, reminding him he would have to work tomorrow. Let me just take Chelsea Laine, and we can talk about all of this tomorrow. I'm going to stay at my parents' house tonight. Of course, we started arguing about all of that. All I wanted to do was get the hell out of there with my baby and deal with things later.

We began to argue, saying the same thing over and over, which was complete insanity, I know. I kept saying to him, "Just let me take Chelsea Laine, and we can talk about all of this tomorrow." And he would say, "No, you're not taking her." Then, with a gun in his hand, he grabbed the back of my shirt and lifted me, sort of dragging me across the house as he was saying, "Fine man, just leave—get the f*ck out of here!"

I walked out to my car, which was right outside the side door. All I could think was, *I am not leaving this house without my baby.*

I was standing next to my car door, extremely upset as things had just become physical. He was standing with the door open to the back of the house with his sawed-off shotgun in his hand. We must have argued, saying the same thing over and over for probably another 15 minutes. I kept telling him that I was going to call the police if he didn't let me take the baby. The conversation was going nowhere. Finally, he said the words to me that would tear my soul apart and cause more damage than anything I had ever experienced in my relationship with him before.

Just like that, out of the mouth of my own husband, who was supposed to love and protect me, came the words, "I will kill you b*tch!" I think I went into some sort of shock. I got into my car and drove down to the end of the street, where there was a Blockbuster video store. For those of you who are not sure what I'm talking about, this was where you rented VHS movies. For some reason, they always had policemen at the store.

I walked into the store, looked at the cop, crying, and said, "Can I please use your telephone?"

He asked me, "Who do you want to call?"

I said, "The police."

He walked me outside and asked me what was wrong. I told him that my husband came home wasted, and he would not let me take our seven-month-old daughter out of the house. I told him what he had said, and he immediately called for backup. He and I drove down to the house and stood on the street. All of a sudden, two police cars came speeding down our street with their lights on. They walked up to the front door, and not a minute or so later, Ben opened the screen door with a sawed-off shotgun hanging straight down from his shoulder! The cops immediately screamed out, *"Gun! Gun!"*

They backed down from the patio, got down on their knees in the grass, and were pointing their guns up toward the door. They asked him to put his hands up. He did, but then slowly stepped back into our home and shut the door. Who could have ever guessed what would happen next? It became a living nightmare. I did not realize any of this at the time, but it had become a hostage situation since he was wasted (out of his mind) and would not release our daughter to me. Soon, two or three SWAT vans came speeding down the street. News reporters and some of our family showed up, as well. I felt like I was living in the middle of a movie.

It seemed as if there were men from the SWAT team behind every other tree in the front and the backyard. Our home was completely surrounded. The police were trying to call the house to try to reason with him, but he would not answer the phone.

Apparently, he was inside the house calling the police, saying, "They're going to kill me, they're going to kill me!" This standoff went on for at least two hours, maybe three—to be honest, I can't remember. Not long after the SWAT team was there, his parents showed up, and so did a reporter from one of the local news channels. The street was filled with people. I didn't even realize it, but the police were in conversation with Ben for over an hour, as they said this was considered a suicide watch.

Since he was not coming out or releasing our daughter, the nightmare continued. A helicopter with an infrared light was flying over our house. In hindsight, I'm honestly surprised that the two cops did not shoot him when I saw him open the door with a gun.

Hours had gone by. It seemed like an eternity. The police finally coerced him into coming outside. Everyone's eyes were glued to the door. At one point, he came out on the front porch very calmly and said, "You can come in now." He took one step back close to the house as if he was listening and then leaned forward and said, "The baby is crying, I'm going to get her a bottle." And he went back into the house, and the standoff continued for probably another 30 minutes.

Finally, after all of the conversations on the phone back and forth, we got him to come out with his hands up. They arrested him and took him to jail. We entered the house immediately. Thankfully, Chelsea Laine was asleep. As we went through the house, it looked completely ransacked from his frantic behavior with those infrared binoculars. It was a nightmare. I took Chelsea Laine and went to my parents' to stay the night.

DISCUSSION QUESTIONS

1. What emotions did Erika experience during the SWAT incident?

2. At what point do you think Erika realized she had to protect not just herself, but her daughter?

3. How do you discern the difference between fear that paralyzes and fear that prompts change?

Devotional Scripture: Psalm 34:4 — *I sought the Lord, and he answered me; he delivered me from all my fears.*

Reflection: God meets us in moments of terror with the courage we don't know we have.

Prayer: Lord, when fear surrounds me, help me turn to You. Give me the strength to act with courage and protect what You've entrusted to me.

CHAPTER EIGHT

LIVING ON THE EDGE

SURROUNDED BY CHAOS

In the next couple of days, Ben got out of jail and came home. I guess his attorney (who was his uncle) or his parents had bailed him out once again. (This was not the first time he had been arrested.)

Are you ready for the crazy-sick part of the story? When he was released from jail, he came home, and I was cooking him dinner. *Was I crazy? Had I lost my mind?* I was extremely confused and hurt!

His sister came to visit and was at our house. She and I normally got along, but that night we got caught up in an argument. She came into our home and was blaming me for his arrest. Can you even imagine how I must have felt? His family had always blamed me for his misbehavior, arrests, etc. She was yelling at me to get out of the house. (Really, me? Get out of *my* house? You have got to be kidding!)

When you are surrounded by chaos, it seems like your body goes into an accelerated fight or flight mode of desperation. Knowing where I am today personally and spiritually, it just blows my mind that I would ever tolerate this behavior and allow myself to stay in such a toxic relationship. If I had known a healthier way to live—and, most importantly, if I had known Jesus personally—I would have recognized Him as my Protector and Savior and cried out to Him. At this time in my life, even though I believed in God, I had no idea how much He could have brought to my life. I could have had such peace, joy, courage, and most of all, I would not have felt like I was doing life alone. If I had known to lean on Him during those crazy times, what would I have done differently?

The next day, we got up, and I tried to act as normal as I could. In trauma, your body and mind tend to go back to a familiar place for survival. It is like you go into autopilot mode to keep the peace and not "rock the boat."

We had a tender moment. I remember sitting on his lap in the spare bedroom. He just cried and apologized. I forgave him once again. At that point, something was different from all of the years of the same cycle of fighting and making up. I said, "You told me that you would kill me! As a matter of fact, you said, 'I'll kill you bitch!' You are my husband; you're supposed to be my protector, and now I'm scared of you."

Of course, he begged and pleaded, saying he was sorry—just like he had so many times before, over and over again. As we were having this conversation, something inside me had snapped, and I could not go back. Maybe it was that I now had my daughter to think about? I had someone else to protect. It wasn't just about me anymore. Or was it that I had learned just enough from church and from my Christian friends at the salon to know better—and that I simply couldn't go back?

A NEW AWARENESS

I believe right around this time, I had bought a book for a client called *Codependent No More* by Melody Beattie. I had heard of this book before, and thought it could maybe help my friend. But when I finally opened it up and started to read a few pages, I started to cry. I said to myself, "This is me!" I knew it was crazy that I stayed with Ben and went back to his behavior over and over, and I didn't know why. This was the start of my new life and learning a healthier way of living. I knew it was time to get off the tormenting treadmill of life I was living. I had to change something in my life to see a change. I had to set up some boundaries to protect myself and my baby. This was the key to unlocking my life to move forward.

As crazy as this sounds, a few months later, we attended a marriage weekend encounter event together in a last-ditch effort to save our marriage, but it was simply too late. We were supposed to have a romantic dinner, and we ended up going to bed early, falling asleep, and missing the dinner. So, after our daughter, Chelsea Laine's first birthday, I moved out of our home in Ft. Worth and into my parents' house in Duncanville, and we proceeded with the divorce.

After making this decision, I was devastated, as you can imagine. I was heartbroken because I never wanted to get divorced. I wanted the freedom to work on my own hours so that I could raise Chelsea Laine and not send her to daycare. My mom was home with us full-time until I was in the third grade, and that's what I wanted to do for my children, as well.

This is probably one of the reasons I didn't want a divorce, so that we would have two incomes, and I would be free to be a stay-at-home mom until she started kindergarten. Was it worth it to leave an abusive and toxic home? Was it hard and scary? Yes, of course—because I finally really knew that he was not going to change. At this point, we had already been together for about 12 years, dated for six, and were married for six, if you were keeping track.

At the beginning of each of our monthly meetings at Hair Logic, we would always be asked the question, "Does anyone have anything they want us to pray for?" While everyone I worked with was sitting in the front of the salon, I said, "Yes."

As I began to speak, I said the words, "It's just..." and then I began to cry. I tried to get a hold of myself, and then I began to speak again, "It's just..." and the tears rolled down my face. I had to walk to the back of the salon to compose myself before trying for the third time to finally get the words out.

"It's just nobody is going to love Ben the way I do." There, I finally said it. I never meant to sound self-righteous, but I seriously felt that if I left him, he just wouldn't survive. You see, when you are sick with codependency, the alcoholic or narcissist finds a way to manipulate you into thinking that they just can't survive without you. They make you their savior. Which is a horrible place to be and completely off track. Only God can be anyone's savior. Putting this kind of pressure on a person is simply sickening and can make you feel debilitated. So the next thing that happened was actually my first experience with deliverance. At the time, I wouldn't have known to call it that, but it is exactly what happened.

SET FREE

One of the ladies who worked there, named Lucia, put her hands on my head, and the girls who worked at the salon all placed themselves around me, and Lucia prayed in the Spirit. I didn't know what was going on at the time. Back then, at the beginning of my spiritual journey, I would have said that this was a little holy roller. However, after they were done praying, the feeling that I was responsible for Ben completely left my soul and never returned. This is what I have come to know as deliverance. It is a simple prayer that released me from feeling as if I were the only one who could help Ben. I was set free that day and never felt guilty for divorcing again! This was one of my very first spiritual miracles.

DISCUSSION QUESTIONS

1. What realization shifted Erika's mindset after reading *"Codependent No More?"*

2. How do unhealthy patterns keep us from experiencing the freedom God desires for us?

3. What would it look like for you to draw a new boundary in your life?

Devotional Scripture: 2 Corinthians 5:17 — *Therefore, if anyone is in Christ, the new creation has come: The old has gone, the new is here!*

Reflection: Healing begins when we see ourselves through God's promise of renewal.

Prayer: Father, thank You for making me new. Help me to walk in freedom and to leave the old patterns behind.

CHAPTER NINE

THE BREAKING POINT

A RAY OF LIGHT IN THE DARK

S hortly after I had left Ben for good, I went with my best friend to a party for a mutual friend in Dallas. We went into the kitchen, and she said, "Erika, there is a new crew member in my husband's band." She continued, "His name is Jason, and he is your type!" I immediately said I was not interested. I mean, I had just left an abusive, toxic relationship and hadn't even considered the thought of dating again. Alas, when we went back outside, I ended up sitting next to him, and I swear, everything that came out of his mouth was like sunshine. (And...yes, he was very cute!) After the going-away party, we all went to Greenville Avenue, an area with many restaurants, little bars, and shops that were close by.

We ended up at a little bar called Muddy Waters. Even though we were there with many friends, Jason and I were drawn to each other and just kept talking and getting to know each other, as if no one else was there. He was staying with Mark around the corner at one of the band members' houses. After the bar closed down, we went over and sat out front in the bed of his truck and talked for hours. One of his best qualities I noticed was that he actually listened to me when I talked, which was something that Ben *never* did. Ben would always leave the room when I was talking or avoid eye contact, which left me feeling unheard or as if my thoughts were not important.

The alternative pop band from Dallas was with Island Records at the time and in the middle of a tour, so Jason was on the road most of the time. But when he was in Dallas on breaks, we would see each other as friends (at first). Jason helped me with things in my house, which I greatly appreciated, and we enjoyed each other's company. His demeanor was calm and kind. I enjoyed his company; he was very comfortable to be around, and one of the coolest things I loved about him was that he was classically trained in piano and would play for me sometimes.

At some point during this time, Ben wrote me a letter that said everything you would ever want to hear from your spouse or from someone who said they loved you. In the past, his letter would have manipulated me to go back to him. This time, though, it was simply too late.

BREAKING THE CYCLE

When you are sick of codependency in a relationship with someone, you tend to have no boundaries, and you always think that things will change. *If only I would do this, it would be better. Maybe I should try responding this way, this time.* I had tried this before, and as patterns were interrupted, things would improve for a short time, only to spiral out of control again, eventually. Truly, it was just a cycle of the same song, different verse.

Codependents often believe that everything is their fault. The book *Codependent No More* helped me to understand that I cannot fix or change anyone. I could pray for Ben. I could encourage him, but nothing would change if he wasn't willing and ready to do so, on his own. We are only responsible for ourselves.

AN ANGEL IN DISGUISE

Even though we didn't have a long-lasting relationship or end up married, I will forever be grateful for Jason. I sincerely feel that had I not met him during that vulnerable time in my life, I may have gone back to Ben! I believe he was an angel sent from God to wake me up and see that life could be different.

DISCUSSION QUESTIONS

1. Have you ever experienced a moment where you felt someone was sent into your life at just the right time? What impact did that have on you?

2. What patterns or relationships in your life have you needed to break free from, and what helped you take that step?

3. How do you recognize the difference between emotional comfort and God-led peace when meeting someone new?

Devotional Scripture: Psalm 34:18 — *The Lord is close to the brokenhearted and saves those who are crushed in spirit.*

Reflection: Sometimes God sends people into our lives not forever, but for a divine purpose—like a lighthouse in the fog. When we feel weakest, He often meets us through the kindness of others who listen, uplift, and gently steer us toward healing.

Prayer: Lord, thank You for the unexpected ways You show up in my life—through people, moments, and even hard endings. Help me to listen for Your voice, trust Your timing, and believe that You are always working for my healing and freedom. Amen.

CHAPTER TEN

PACKING UP THE PIECES

FINDING MY OWN PLACE

As soon as I could afford it, I quit my job at the salon in Arlington and Chelsea Laine and I moved from my parents' house in Duncanville to East Dallas in a triplex on Victor Street, near one of my best friends' houses. It was *everything* to me to have our own place where we could start over and have a peaceful home far away from the day-to-day chaos I had been living in.

A couple of months later, one of my other best friends (the one that I had moved in with when I thought I was leaving Ben the first time) from childhood moved into the place right next door. This was very comforting since Chelsea Laine and I were on our own.

My next job was at Warren Raymond Salon on McKinney Avenue. The area is now known as UpTown, which is right outside of downtown Dallas. The salon was a really cool place to work, with upbeat music and a contemporary style. The people who worked there were really nice, as were the clients. After Warren hired me,

I met Teel, who was the receptionist. She was beautiful, fun, and so full of life.

Eric and Bobby were the hairstylists at the salon; if you were anyone, you went to them for your hair color and cuts. We all got to know each other fairly quickly and had a blast at work. We sometimes went out clubbing and dancing on the weekends when Ben would have Chelsea Laine. At this time, Ben had standard visitation, which meant that he would pick her up on Friday night at six o'clock and bring her home on Sunday evening at six o'clock every 1st, 3rd, and 5th weekends.

I was 26 years old, trying to get in the groove of being a single parent, which was challenging as the sole breadwinner. Before our divorce was finalized, which took a full year, Ben contributed nothing financially—because he didn't have to! Later, I found out that I could have filed a *temporary order* (or something like that) and would have been eligible to receive child support even while going through the divorce. It would have been a game-changer had I known this information. When we were finally divorced, I received an inconsistent $250 in child support monthly. While it was something, it sure wasn't enough.

Ben continued to try to control me despite our divorce. Frequently, on his visitation weekends, he would use Chelsea Laine as a way to ruin my plans with friends by deciding to randomly drop her back off with me several hours early. We would argue about it, making it uncomfortable for everyone around me. It put me right back into the whirlwind of feeling trapped and helpless.

LEARNING TO SET BOUNDARIES

Finally, my best friend (who I was with all the time) said, "Don't listen to him, your divorce papers say that he will drop her back off at your house at 6:00 p.m. He's not just going to leave her on your doorstep!" Before this encouragement, I would have simply dropped everything and bowed to Ben's demands. This time, though, I listened to her advice, and it worked! That day, I showed up at my apartment at 6:00 p.m. on the dot.

Just as she said, Ben was there with our daughter at the correct time. I finally realized this was just another scheme and form of control. In the future, I decided to stop responding to his controlling demands. This type of communication with requests and requirements is called "healthy boundaries." Remember, you cannot fix or change the person, but you *can* change how *you respond*. This is a *huge* lesson you will learn as you walk down the path of being set free from codependency.

Ben would also occasionally call me and ask if I could keep Chelsea Laine on Friday nights during his regularly scheduled visitation times. You see, it wasn't so much that he needed me to keep her during his visitation; it was more about control and not allowing me to make plans of my own. So, after I did this a few times, I started practicing my boundaries and said, "No, you will have to figure it out on your own." It wasn't that I didn't want to keep Chelsea Laine during "his hours"—actually, I would have loved to just have her all the time—but I knew his request was much more than that.

If I'm being honest, it actually killed me to say no—I felt guilty. After all, this is my *daughter*. However, when you stand your ground with a manipulator, everything changes. I know this may seem crazy, but when you have put up with constant chaos for so long and one day you break free of it, your whole life changes. I felt a sense of freedom for the first time; I finally wasn't being controlled. I realized that, though I was divorced, somehow, I was still allowing Ben to manipulate me into unnecessary things. Having this mental clarity changed everything for me.

A VILLAGE IN THE CITY

Eric, one of my close friends and somebody whom I adored at the Warren Raymond Salon, told me about some new apartments in Deep Ellum that offered rent on a sliding scale. At first, I was opposed to what I thought was government housing. I know that government housing can be a blessing to some, but I had it in my head that it would not be a nice place. I had grown up in the nice part of town and didn't want to depend on the government for help. I soon found out, though, that it was nothing of the sort. They were actually luxury apartments owned by Jefferson Properties, which was a family-owned and operated company. The company had made a deal with the city of Dallas to offer ten percent of their properties on a sliding scale in exchange for the apartment complex not paying property tax for ten years.

It turned out to be a Godsend, and in 1997, Chelsea Laine and I moved into our first Jefferson property. It was a brand new, 1,250 square foot apartment at a price that I could afford. I felt very fortunate to have learned about this program. It was the city of Dallas' way of getting people to move into the city. Dallas has grown so much since I lived there, so I guess their plan worked.

Ten percent of the renters ended up being single moms. This was really cool because I met several of them, and we became our own tight-knit community. One of the single moms was named Shun. She was getting her degree from Southern Methodist University in Highland Park, about five miles from downtown Dallas. I was very impressed. One of her daughters, Aerial, was a couple of years older than Chelsea Laine, and they became best friends. Aerial later told us that she would see Chelsea Laine riding around on her scooter and see us coming and going in and out of the car and said, "Y'all looked like you were having so much fun, and I wanted to know y'all!"

When Jefferson Properties built a new complex less than five miles away, we both moved. It was so much fun; the girls loved playing together, and it was great support for us moms. Shun even talked me into going to college at El Centro, but that only lasted one semester.

Do you remember me telling you about Donna, who owned Clippers Inn in Lawton, Oklahoma? Well, her daughter Michelle ended up moving to Dallas with her son Tyler, who was only a year older than Chelsea Laine. They went to the same schools at first, so Michelle and I tagged team responsibilities and joked that we were each other's "husbands."

Chelsea Laine and I went on to live at two other Jefferson Properties. The first one was at Gaston Yard, in the Deep Ellum entertainment district known for its vibrant street murals, quirky art galleries, and longtime concert venues for music such as indie and blues. Brewpubs, cocktail bars, Tex-Mex eateries, and one of our favorite restaurants, St. Pete's Dancing Marlin, lined the sides of the streets.

The next apartment was by American Airlines Arena; then we moved to Bryan Place. When Jefferson Properties would build a new property, there were incentives to move into them, and for me, it was just exciting to be in a fresh new place. I cannot tell you what it meant to be in such a luxury apartment that gave single moms a chance to provide a beautiful and safe place for their families. Chelsea Laine and I lived in the Downtown Dallas area for around eight years.

When we weren't dealing with all of this drama from her dad, Chelsea Laine and I had a fun life. I always threw the most fun birthday parties for her at a hotel so that she and her friends could swim and have a slumber party. Even though I was on a budget, I always found a way to make things fun!

Her friend Aeriel was always impressed that I allowed half of the living room to become "Barbie Land." It was behind the couch, and it didn't matter because when you came in the front door, all you could see was our pretty living room.

DISCUSSION QUESTIONS

1. What boundaries in your life do you need to create or strengthen, and how might those boundaries bring peace?

2. How can your home—whether small or grand—become a sanctuary of safety, growth, and joy?

3. When have you discovered strength in community, even when it came from an unexpected place?

Devotional Scripture: Proverbs 14:1 — *The wise woman builds her house, but with her own hands the foolish one tears hers down.*

Reflection: A peaceful home is a powerful testimony. When we begin to reclaim our space from fear and chaos, we allow God to restore what was broken and fill our lives with joy.

Prayer: Lord, thank You for being the builder of every strong foundation. Teach me to protect the peace in my life and home. Help me to stand firm in the boundaries You've led me to create, and let my home reflect Your love, stability, and joy. Amen.

CHAPTER ELEVEN

RUNNING TOWARD SAFETY

THE NORDSTROM YEARS

I n 1997, I took a job in the cosmetics department at Nordstrom, an upscale department store at the Galleria in Dallas, which is a three-level mall with department stores, dining, an ice skating rink, and a hotel all under one roof. I have had a love for cosmetics, skincare, and makeup since I was in high school. As an aesthetician and makeup artist, I really loved working at Nordstrom. I also appreciated that their handbook had only one rule: *Use your good judgment in all situations*. This gave me the freedom to give the best customer service I could, and my personality was able to shine. I loved being around all of the latest fashions and makeup trends.

On one of my breaks, I wandered over to the jewelry counter and saw a beautiful watch that I just loved. It was a Michele Deco Mid Diamond and Mother of Pearl Dial Watch in stainless steel.

I could never afford a watch of such luxury as a single mom, but I would daydream of wearing it.

One day during one of my shifts, Ben, his girlfriend Bonnie, and Chelsea Laine stopped by to see me at work since their apartment was just around the corner. I suppose Chelsea Laine was asking to see me. After their short visit, Chelsea Laine began to cry and said she wanted to go back home with me. She was only three years old at the time, and this completely wrecked me! I had to wonder what was going on over at her dad's place that she, at age three, was clinging to my legs and crying that she wanted to stay with me. Did she feel scared or unsafe? It was hard to tell with her being so young and unable to express more details of why she was feeling this way.

A TRAP IN THE PARKING GARAGE

When I left work, I went into the parking garage to my car, and I noticed a note on my windshield. It was a note from Ben telling me that I could come by their apartment to pick her up and allowing me to have her overnight. I was so excited and relieved! I drove as fast as I could and let them know that I was there so that they could bring her down to my car. I waited five minutes… then ten… then fifteen. *What is going on?* They kept saying they were getting Chelsea Laine's things together and they'd be just a minute. After twenty-plus minutes, I noticed police lights coming toward me. *Ben and Bonnie had called the police!* I showed the officer the note Ben had given to come to his house, and I soon realized that it had been a trap. There was always something fishy going on. By now, I believe he had a terrible addiction, and his actions showed it, so this led him to be very paranoid.

Eventually, Bonnie and Ben brought Chelsea Laine out to the car, and she got to come with me for the night. Although it was wonderful having her for the night, it was terrifying not knowing what was going on over there, or what she would be going back to when she returned the next day, based on the stories Chelsea Laine would tell me about when she was with her dad. It just was not a stable or healthy environment for her to be in.

As a side note to all of this, it seemed that Ben's family was continuously trying to prove that I was an unfit mom for no reason other than drama. Meanwhile, it was a struggle for him to pay the child support that he had agreed to in the court order. Rarely did he help out in any other way, such as with medical needs or extra-curricular activities that would come up. Even when I would take Chelsea Laine to the doctor, he was supposed to pay back half of the incurred bill, but it was always a struggle to get him to reimburse me, and most of the time, he never did.

When Chelsea Laine was four years old, I registered her in a private school. It offered great academics as well as music class, piano lessons, swimming, dance class, and horse riding on Fridays. She wore an adorable navy blue and white uniform. I felt really comfortable having her at this school, even though it was probably out of my budget and a 25-minute commute in traffic each way. Still, there was nothing I wouldn't do to give her the best in education and environment. My friend Michelle had her son enrolled at the same school, and we continued to support each other by sharing carpooling responsibilities, which helped immensely.

SEARCHING FOR SAFETY AND STABILITY

Later, I heard that there was a public school off of Mockingbird called Stonewall Jackson Elementary that was highly revered as a blue ribbon, exemplary school. As much as I liked the private school, Stonewall Jackson was closer, and it was *free*! To a single mom who was only getting $250 in child support, that was a big deal. There was only one problem: you had to live in the district to attend there, and we lived in downtown Dallas. My mom was nice enough to move into the district off of Greenville Avenue so that we could use her address. Her house was really close to the school, so when I had early call times at AMS Productions, where I was a makeup artist for TV and film, I could drop her off at my mom's, and she would get her to school. If I had to work late, she could also pick her up from school. It was a really great situation, and it brought me much comfort. I will forever be grateful for her help, love, and support with Chelsea Laine.

Chelsea Laine's first-grade teacher was named Mrs. Williamson, and she was absolutely wonderful. I remember that the kids had a garden to tend to, which I thought was really cool and unique to have at a public school.

On Chelsea Laine's first-grade field day event, Ben came to support her. I had not seen him in a while because we had changed his visitation hours so that he would pick up Chelsea Laine from school on Friday and drop her back at school on Monday morning. This kept him in line a little better than when we had to meet to make the exchange. We always had to change the order of the divorce decree so that I could be protected and not controlled by his actions.

When I saw him that day, I was kind of in shock. Ben had lost a lot of weight and looked terrible. He was normally very fit, so this was alarming. He had been back on drugs for a while, which made all of the weird things that Chelsea Laine had been telling me finally make sense.

He even asked Mrs. Williamson to go on a date! It was so uncomfortable and embarrassing. Even she could tell that something was off with Ben. He always acted narcissistically, to say the least.

Can you imagine learning that your ex-husband was on drugs and you still had to let your child go with him for his visitation and couldn't really do much about it? I think my adrenaline was always on overdrive with worry. I wanted to hire an attorney, but it simply was not in my budget. I researched and reached out to several government agencies to see if there was a way I could get his parental rights revoked, but every time it was a no-go.

During the next couple of years, Chelsea Laine attended Stonewall Jackson Elementary. I was not comfortable having her go with her dad every other weekend, but I had no choice, despite how eerie I felt about it.

Since I couldn't figure out how to get his parental rights revoked, I sought out other ways of support and found some peace while attending church in North Dallas. We attended Prestonwood Baptist Church for about a year, and I even sent Chelsea Laine to summer camp with their youth department that year. During this season of life, we built a few meaningful friendships at Prestonwood Baptist Church that truly ministered to us. While we weren't deeply connected with many people there and mostly just attended services, those few friendships were a real blessing.

DISCUSSION QUESTIONS:

1. What environments or jobs have helped you rediscover your strengths?

2. When have you experienced an emotional "trap" or manipulative situation? How did you (or could you) rely on faith or wisdom to navigate it?

3. What sacrifices have you made (or seen others make) in pursuit of providing safety and stability for loved ones?

Devotional Scripture: Psalm 9:9 — *The Lord is a refuge for the oppressed, a stronghold in times of trouble.*

Reflection: Sometimes our greatest testimonies are formed in the middle of survival—not success. It's in these moments that God becomes our true stronghold.

Prayer: Lord, when life feels unfair and overwhelming, be my safe place. Strengthen me to stand firm in love, wisdom, and discernment. Help me to protect those I love and trust that You see every injustice and will carry me through. Amen.

CHAPTER TWELVE

CAUGHT BETWEEN FAITH AND FEAR

PLAYING DRESS-UP OR HIDING IN PLAIN SIGHT

All through Chelsea Laine's third-grade year, Ben continued to be unreliable and unpredictable. He was behind on child support, moved frequently, and lost his white Corvette due to repossession. Chelsea Laine also told me that her dad was dressing up when he went to take out the trash, so that the "bad men from work" would not recognize him. Hearing stories like this terrified me for Chelsea Laine. *What was he hiding... Money? Drugs? Or did he owe money for drugs?* I kept asking myself *how any judge in his right mind would order a child to spend time alone with a parent involved in so much foul play?* Still, my hands were tied, and I felt helpless. Thankfully, Chelsea Laine was young enough that she didn't seem to be frightened at all by his behavior; she thought he was truly just playing dress up. That was God's grace.

During this time, I found out that Ben was living with a room-mate named Gary in Arlington. I found a way to get Gary's phone number as I was desperate to find out more. He told me that Ben had put up cameras in the front entryway of the house and was act-ing really strange and paranoid. He was doing meth and who knows what else at this time, or so I heard, and Gary was scared of him. So, he made up a story that they needed to move out just to get Ben out of the house! Gary even went so far as to move all of his belongings out of the house just to make Ben think that he was moving, and when Ben left, Gary moved back in.

HIRING AN ATTORNEY

By now, there were so many things that didn't add up that I was des-perately seeking help. One of my best friend's sisters knew all about my struggle, and she told me that she knew a good attorney. Even though it was financially impossible to afford to hire an attorney, I trusted my friend's suggestion and, in desperation, reached out to the attorney. Something in my gut told me to take action and pro-tect Chelsea Laine. At the time, I didn't understand that God was whispering in my spirit, but now I know it was just that. Polly Rae O'Toole graciously agreed to represent me for a low retainer fee and a small monthly payment. I knew this was not nearly enough to cover her fees—she was one of the best in the area—but I believe she was an angel sent from God. I didn't know how I would squeeze in another bill, but I was desperate, so I agreed to the terms. I just prayed and asked God to provide for us during this time.

The following weekend, when I was visiting one of my close friends, Tammy, I got up enough courage to ask if she would help me pay the $1,000 down payment to my attorney. I'll never forget how she immediately walked right to her closet, grabbed her purse, and wrote out a check. I cannot tell you how much that meant to me. As embarrassing as it was, I was fighting for my daughter, and I was, and still am, so grateful for the understanding, love, and comfort that this money provided. I finally felt as if I had a chance in protecting Chelsea Laine.

A BAD CHECK AND A FROZEN ACCOUNT

During this time, I was working as a medical aesthetician at Medical City in Dallas for a plastic surgeon. I really loved this job. I was in charge of skin care sales, facials, and medical treatments, and sometimes I got to observe liposuction, breast augmentation, and tummy tucks. I was number one in sales in the Dallas area for our private label skin care line that would later become a company called Revision (a cosmeceutical skin care), and number three in sales for OBAGI, a medical grade skin care. I was really doing well and felt as if my career was on the right track. I was finally able to pay all of my bills and was feeling pretty proud of myself. I had opened a bank account in the lobby of the building, which made it very convenient. Many of the ladies who worked there were my clients. One day, my coworkers and I went to the food court for our lunch break. I went to pay for my lunch with my debit card, and it was declined. I was instantly embarrassed and worried. Last I had checked, my account balance was $1,300. Since my bank was just steps away, I told the girls I'd be right back, that I wanted to check on my bank account.

The teller looked up my account and said, "The bank has frozen your account." I remember her sitting there with her hands clasped, me on the edge of my seat with fear. My heart sank. She told me that I had deposited a check for $1,250 (a back child support check that Ben had given me), and it was flagged as suspicious. I had no idea what to think.

She said, "To the bank, it appears that you were trying to launder money." I began to cry out of disbelief, embarrassment, and complete disappointment. *I don't even know how to launder money! What is happening?!* Apparently, the check was from an account that didn't exist anymore—a joint account from when Ben and I were married eight years previously. The check he gave me only had his name on it, but in the bank records, I was also on the account.

As a backstory, when I had received the check several days prior, I had called the credit union from which it came and asked the banker about this check. I didn't recognize it, so I was trying to find out what account this was from and if the check was good. There had been so many things going on with Ben that I didn't trust him. By now, he was without a job, a car, and was living back at his parents' house.

They told me that there were no funds available. What they didn't tell me was that the account had been closed. When I called my attorney about the situation, she told me to go ahead and deposit it so we would have proof that he was writing bad checks for his child support. Then it would be documented for our case. She had instructed me, of course, to not write anything against the balance, and so I followed her instructions. How could we have known that this check was written from an account that didn't even exist anymore? Besides, I knew I had $1,300 of my own hard-earned cash in the bank, so I knew I was financially secure.

I had a credit card that was for overdraft protection, so I would never have overdraft fees if my account got close to a zero balance before my next paycheck. However, the bank used my overdraft protection credit card to pay for this bad check, and my backup plan was gone. I had no clue that was going to happen!

Memories of my childhood flashed through my mind. My father was a dad who followed through with his word. He was someone

I could trust to be honest, hardworking, and a provider. It was so heavy on my heart that my daughter had such an unfit father.

To add insult to injury, when I got in my car to head home, I realized that I needed gas. I couldn't use my debit card, and I had no credit cards or cash. I went into panic mode. What in the world was I going to do? I couldn't make it back home unless I got gas—the low fuel light had come on as I drove to work that morning. There was a station right across the street from my work, so I pulled in and had to do what I had to do. I pulled up to the pump and waited to get up my nerve to ask someone if they could please put five dollars' worth of gas in my tank. I had my scrubs on and was looking very professional. I was so embarrassed!

I proceeded to tell a woman at the pump that I worked at Medical City at a doctor's office and I had forgotten my bank card, or something like that. I told her that if she would give me her address, I would mail her the money back. She said, "Don't worry about it." I was so grateful for her kindness. I know that this may not seem like a big deal, but it traumatized me. I went from feeling on top of the world with my career to feeling like a loser and a nobody, all because of one bad check. Unfortunately, this was only the beginning. This began the downward spiral that led to my financial ruin.

THE CALL THAT CHANGED EVERYTHING

Ring. Ring.

"Hello?"

"Hi Erika. It's Sybil," my ex-mother-in-law's voice said on the other end of the line. "Are you sitting down?"

I immediately got a knot in my stomach. "Wh-what's going on?"

"We just got in a big knock-down, drag-out fight with Ben," Sybil said. "He took off with Chelsea Laine, and we don't know where they are going."

"*Left?!*" I said in shock. "With who?"

"With a guy named Scott," she said. "They were in his truck."

"You don't have any idea where they would be going?" I asked.

"No."

No. Left. Gone. Chelsea Laine. As I hung up the phone, I began to cry. Trying to think optimistic thoughts, I tried to not panic. *Surely,* I thought, *Ben will call his mother or me soon, and everything will be okay.* My whole body felt frozen, some kind of shock, I suppose. I sat there by the phone, willing myself not to panic and trying to believe that my eight-year-old wasn't kidnapped; she was just with her father.

I already knew that Ben was on a rapid downward spiral, and this just confirmed what I feared—he was not on a good path. Still, under Texas law, I felt helpless to protect Chelsea Laine from being with him during his court-ordered visitation. And now, my night-mares were becoming reality. As is fairly standard with joint custody following divorces, the father typically gets routine weekends and one full month of visitation during the summer. While I was still worried sick because of the circumstances, and though I never really felt comfortable with Chelsea Laine being with Ben for an entire month anyway, I had no choice. I told myself that he still had a couple of weeks left of his summer visitation, and they were just on a trip. I just had to rely on God for strength.

CHELSEA LAINE CALLS

A painful two days went by before I received a call. *Ring. Ring.*

"Hi, Mom!"

I tried to conceal the panic in my voice, and probably a little too upbeat, I said, "Hi, Punky! Where are you?"

Her voice seemed carefree as she answered, "Oh, we're in a motel!"

"In a motel… Where?" I asked.

"Dad, where are we?"

In the background, I heard him respond, "Arlington."

"We're in Arlington, Mom."

I let out a breath of relief knowing she was only 30 minutes away. "So what's going on?" I asked. "Where are y'all going?"

"I'm not sure," she said.

"Are you ok?"

She answered back, "Ya, Mom, I'm fine."

A few days later, Chelsea Laine called again to tell me that she was staying at Aunt Kira's house, which was in Grand Prairie, about 25 minutes from our home. I just had to see her for myself to make sure she was ok. I asked her if she had been taking her allergy medication.

"No, we ran out."

A-ha! A way in. Every time she would stop taking her allergy medication, she would end up with bronchitis or strep, so I told her that I would bring it to her. The next day, I stopped by Kira's house, honked the horn, and she came out. When she walked outside to meet me, I wanted to break down and cry. She looked like a mess. Her teeth weren't brushed, her hair was knotted, and she had cat hair all over her clothes. My first instinct was to put her in my car and leave, but then I knew that would go against our divorce decree and cause more trouble. I was also a little scared of the situation and what would happen if I took her without Ben knowing. I talked to her as long as I could, hugged her as I cried, and said goodbye. I questioned my sanity when I drove away, but left it in God's hands.

A few days later, I spoke with Kira. Chelsea Laine had been basically dropped off at her house while Ben was out gallivanting around. As we talked, she told me that she had found a wig, two locked briefcases, and a gun. I remembered Chelsea Laine's story about Ben dressing up to take out the trash, and it was clear that he was on the run from something or somebody. I began to second-guess myself for not taking Chelsea Laine home when I had the chance earlier that week. Kira told me that she was scared of Ben; he was hard and fast into drugs, and she never knew what to expect. Apparently, he had somehow gotten a cell phone through her account without her permission.

Also, around that time, a friend of mine from high school, Marsha, told me that she could swear that she saw Ben at a nightclub in the Arlington area. The person she was talking to was wearing makeup and dressed as a woman, but she said, "I know it was him!" Our lives were spinning out of control! Can you even imagine the worry I must have had trying to go to work and be fully there, feeling as if my child had been kidnapped? It was unimaginable to say the least.

Looking back, that season was a whirlwind of fear, desperation, and survival. Yet even in the darkest moments—when I had no control and everything felt like it was falling apart—God's hand was steady. He sent the right people, provided unexpected help, and gave me just enough strength to face each day. What looked like chaos to me was still fully in His hands. And while I couldn't always protect Chelsea Laine on my own, I had to trust the One who loved her even more than I did.

DISCUSSION QUESTIONS

1. How did Erika demonstrate courage and resourcefulness during this turbulent time?

2. In what ways did God provide for Erika through people and circumstances?

3. When have you faced a situation that felt completely out of control, and how did you hold onto faith?

Devotional Scripture: Psalm 46:1 — *God is our refuge and strength, an ever-present help in trouble.*

Reflection: Even when we feel powerless, God is present. He equips us to protect what He's entrusted to us.

Prayer: God, when fear overwhelms and I don't know what to do, help me turn to You. Give me wisdom, strength, and peace as I fight for what matters most.

PART III

BREAKING THE CHAINS

CHAPTER THIRTEEN

WHISPERS OF STRENGTH

CALLING FOR HELP THAT NEVER CAME

After all the uneasy incidents and lack of stability, I had no other choice but to call the authorities. I called the police and Child Protective Services and explained the situation to them. To my dismay, I did not receive the help that I desperately needed. They just said that it was Ben's right to have his daughter since it was his visitation month. This was a dead-end, dire situation.

I remember during this time reflecting back on a trip to Playa Del Carmen that Chelsea Laine and I had taken. One of my dear friends, Shannon, with whom I had grown up with, needed a nanny to go on their family vacation, and they asked if I was up for it. She said Chelsea Laine was welcome to come along. We had a great time, and I felt very fortunate to be able to go on an all-expenses-paid vacation even though I was working. It really didn't feel much like "work" as I loved little ones, and I had Chelsea Laine with me as well.

One of the days that we were there, I met a lady at the beach who was a single mother. She was telling me a little of her story, and I could read between the lines that she had moved there to run from a dangerous situation with the child's father. She even told me that she was able to legally change their name. Her story was always in the back of my mind. *Could I run away to keep Chelsea Laine safe?* Since I was getting nowhere with the authorities, the thought stayed close to my mind, but it never happened.

I enlisted the wisdom of my good friend Ana. Together, we devised a plan to get Chelsea Laine back safely. Ana called Ben and asked if he would allow her to pick up Chelsea Laine for the day so that they could go to the water park. He agreed! This gave me at least some temporary relief knowing that Chelsea Laine was safe with Ana and her family. When Ana met with Ben to return Chelsea Laine, she said that he was driving a full-sized SUV, a Chevy Tahoe. I had never seen this vehicle or known any of his friends or family to have it. So, I was a bit suspicious, to say the least. Where did this vehicle come from? Ben told Ana that it was his new vehicle. Believe it or not, I still had to wait a week or so to get Chelsea Laine back. When it was finally time to get her back, I was so nervous! I wanted to scream when I saw him and say, *What were you doing?! You idiot! I have been worried sick!*

I tried to stay calm, but I found myself shaking from all of the stress and sheer excitement of getting Chelsea Laine back safely. I was trying to see his driver's license plates in my rearview window, but I was shaking so much I could barely write.

This incident and the next several unexplainable occurrences to follow were the beginning of a complete and total unending nightmare that lasted for the next five years.

HIRING A PRIVATE INVESTIGATOR

During all of this time, my mother and dear friend Ana were helping me keep up with Ben's whereabouts. I received very strange phone calls from unknown people asking for Ben or how to get hold of him. Thankfully, Ana knew a private investigator. The PI went over to Ben's new location in Arlington and staked out the apartment to see if he could obtain information for me. He even knocked on the door, but Ben would not answer, even though the PI knew he was home. The PI found out that the guy Ben was living with and running around with was a known drug dealer. It turns out, it was also the individual Ben had left with when he disappeared with Chelsea Laine. It was all coming together. I felt as if my life was on hold. Other than working, all of my energy was focused on where Ben was and what he was up to. We were moving in the right direction, but I still felt helpless.

SAN ANTONIO TRIP

Chelsea Laine finally came back from her summer visitation with her dad, and I was determined to never let her go back with him. There were too many strange occurrences going on, and I needed to protect my nine-year-old daughter. The next weekend that Ben was supposed to have Chelsea Laine, we took the opportunity. We flew to San Antonio for a family member's wedding. We were safe at least for that weekend. I left a note on the door telling him that as soon as he got settled in his own place, he could have her back. I was just telling him this to buy some time and try to keep him from getting angry. When he drove over to our apartment in downtown Dallas to pick her up and found the note on the door, he was furious. My phone started ringing continually over and over. I did not pick up the phone. He just kept leaving me messages saying that I could have at least told him before he drove across town (a whole 30 minutes). The messages he left began to get more aggressive, cussing me out and threatening me. Ben had a past history of violence and anger issues, so I knew the only way to be safe was to not be anywhere in sight.

During our trip, Chelsea Laine's best friend went to our apartment to take care of our Persian cat. When she got there, she saw terrible writing all over the door. It was like a Charles Manson situation. She called us immediately about the strange message written creepily in red lipstick. This was frightening and unsettling.

When we returned to Dallas from our weekend in San Antonio, to say that I was scared would be an understatement. I had no clue how he might retaliate because I had kept her from him on his weekend. I mean, they were on the run on his last visitation—what would you have done? I called the Dallas police department and told them about the strange occurrences. I asked if they would please come over and make sure we got into our apartment safely from the parking garage to our apartment, but they refused. They just kept saying, "If you see him or he does something to you, then we can help!" *Wow...* That is not what I wanted to hear.

I lived in extreme fear. I was terrified Ben would be around a hallway corner or in my parking garage. I even looked out at my courtyard one time and thought I saw him standing there. Paranoia? Anxiety? I guess it was all the above. All the while, I was trying to seem as normal as I could for Chelsea Laine's sake. This took a lot of self-discipline and courage. I also took out some life insurance in case Ben killed me. Yes, I really thought this was possible, and I needed to have some money set aside for her. Since I had decided to not allow her to go back with Ben on his assigned weekends, I would try to find ways to be away from our apartment. We had lots of friends close by and spent as much time with them as possible.

Our lives were not our own for much of the summer; we weren't really living—we were just surviving, one day at a time. My mom, Ana, and I were working tirelessly, doing our own investigative work as well as working alongside the hired private investigator to find out any evidence that could help us put Ben in jail so that we could finally feel protected. We knew that he was not in a good place in his life and that he was probably on the run from someone, but we needed more information and solid evidence to make a case that the authorities would actually listen to. I was doing all of this while working, trying to keep our home as happy, healthy, and as normal as possible. Chelsea Laine did not know of our day-to-day investigations, so I felt like I was living a double life just trying to keep everything straight. It was summertime, so thankfully, she was blissfully unaware, enjoying her summer with friends and family.

Our days consisted of handling so many details, talking with investigators, police, and credit card companies, handling phone calls that came in from people and businesses looking for Ben, and just trying to work hard to pay the bills. I was totally on my own now with finances, hustling and doing the best I could to keep it all together emotionally. Undoubtedly, this was a huge challenge. My mom was there to help out from time to time, and I had some good friends who I will forever be grateful for their financial help, love, and encouragement during this most difficult time. There's not a day that goes by that I don't remember their kindness.

During this same time, there was a murder that was blasted all over the Dallas news channels. A man had shot and killed his children at his loft in Deep Ellum, only a couple of miles from our apartment. Apparently, the man's ex-wife had been complaining to police about him over and over, but because of her court order, she still had to allow her children to go with him for his scheduled weekend visits. Then one night, he called his ex-wife on the phone and started an argument, and then proceeded to shoot both of their children as the mother helplessly listened to the gunshots on the other end of the phone. Think about how helpless she must have felt! Scared and terrified of what she thought she had heard. It is simply unimaginable! Police said that he left his murdered children in his loft apartment, hopped on an elevator, went down onto the streets and into a bar, and ordered a drink.

I later heard the Judge who presided over their case made a public apology. All of this could have been prevented if he had listened when the mother originally called. And… Here I was going against the law by not allowing Chelsea Laine to see her dad on his regularly scheduled visitation. *Over my dead body* (pun intended) was I going to let her go with him–especially after hearing this story. I actually never truly felt as though he would hurt Chelsea Laine, because she was his only pawn left with which to control me. I actually felt that, if anything, he would kill me so he could have Chelsea Laine all to himself. Maybe in some twisted, codependent way, I was still trying to give him the benefit of the doubt.

RUNNING OUT OF OPTIONS

Ultimately, I decided Chelsea Laine and I needed to just get out of Dallas entirely. Two of my best friends, Alice and Hailey, purchased tickets for Chelsea Laine and me to fly to New York City to hide out for the remainder of the summer. Hailey lived in a loft apartment there, and it was her idea to graciously allow us to move in with her and her husband for the summer. I was working freelance at the time, so I was able to leave. It was summer, and Chelsea Laine was out of school. I couldn't believe this was our life, on the run from an ex-husband I had divorced eight years earlier! I was scared to death of what we would find out in and through our continued and tireless investigation. My friends and I spent hours on the phone trying to find out as much information as possible. We had a suspicion that the Chevy Tahoe that Ben had been driving a few weeks before was stolen, but now we had to prove it. This was our only chance for safety. If we could prove all the illegal things that Ben was involved in, then we would have enough evidence to change the divorce decree. Or, even better, he would be put in jail, and we wouldn't have to worry about what he might do to us.

Being in New York was refreshing. Even though it was under strange circumstances, we tried to enjoy ourselves. Hailey's apartment was in Williamsburg, and I tried to make it as fun as possible for Chelsea Laine. Hailey and her husband were newlyweds, so it was an amazing and kind gesture that they offered for us to come and stay with them. Everyone knew the seriousness of our issues, so they were willing to help out. Most days we hung out at the loft, but some days we got out and rode the L train into Union Park. It was really cool and only two stops to Manhattan.

One of our other classmates, who we knew from Duncanville High, was in town, and one day we all hopped on a train to go out to Coney Island. It was just like I saw on TV or in movies! It had an old-school feel with carnival rides, including the *Cyclone* and *Deno's Wonder Wheel*, and of course, we had a famous Nathan's Hot Dog! It was so much fun to be free of worry and stress for a change.

Before we left Dallas, I had simply told Chelsea Laine that we were going to visit her Aunt Hailey and asked, "Doesn't that sound fun?" I did tell her that she couldn't tell her dad where we were going. She has always been an old soul, so she just seemed to understand and trust what I was saying and had no problem following my lead.

After we were in New York for a few days, I decided to tell Chelsea Laine why we were actually in New York City for an extended vacation. She had no idea that we were basically on the run! I told her that the reason we were there was that we suspected her dad had stolen identities, stolen the Tahoe he had been driving, among other things. She didn't have much to say when I told her, but when she woke up the next morning, she sat straight up in bed and said, "Hey Mom, I know what kind of birthday party I want to have this year."

I said, "What kind?"

She said, "A detective party. All of my friends will have to bring a play car, their mom or dad's driver's license, and a credit card!" Then we died laughing together for several minutes. This was our release and way of coping with this crazy situation. We always found a way to laugh and get through the toughest times. I tried to always tell her the facts without all the drama. I believe this is so important. Many people think that it's necessary to not tell a child anything that may be going on, but I disagree. I believe that being honest and not keeping them completely in the dark about serious situations is the healthiest way to handle these tough situations. However, it is helpful to keep your feelings and emotions out of the story as best you can for their sake. It is not the easiest thing to do, but I believe you will help your child understand and be able to adjust to anything that comes their way. Even though she was only nine at the time, it was important to me to be honest and respect her as a human being.

Ben tried to call and left messages on my cell phone (at the time, there was no such thing as text messaging). I only answered a few of his calls while we were there in New York. I sent a few emails to let him know we were doing fine and that I would get back to him soon. This gave me, my mom, and Ana the time we needed to continue our investigation. We were still spending tireless hours investigating, and since the authorities didn't seem to be nearly as concerned as we were, the load was entirely on me, my mom, and my friends. School was going to start again soon for Chelsea Laine, and we would need to head back to Dallas. My goal was to either get the divorce decree changed by court order before school started, or to find enough evidence that Ben would be arrested, or both, so that Chelsea Laine wouldn't have to go back to her father. We simply didn't have any time to waste.

THE STOLEN TAHOE

Between my mom, the private investigator, Ana, and me, we continued to try to prove that the Tahoe that Ben had been driving was not his, but was, in actuality, stolen. We called police stations, junk yards, and more, as well as talked to other private investigators who were already working on a few stolen identity cases. This process went on for a few weeks, and finally, we heard from the Richardson Police Station. They confirmed for us what we suspected: the Tahoe had indeed been stolen. *Finally...*We now had the evidence that we needed to ensure our safety. Apparently, a lady had picked Ben out of a lineup, but told police that he wasn't bald as shown in the lineup picture. The day he went to test drive the Tahoe, he had worn a wig and a ball cap and told the lady that he wanted to see how the radio sounded. He asked if he could drive it on his own. She complied, and he never returned. He had changed out the license plates; they were apparently from a salvage yard, and they belonged to a doctor in the area. As crazy as it all seemed, we were all relieved and grateful to learn the news. This was the evidence that we needed and had been working on. We could finally move forward, knowing soon we would be safe from all of these shenanigans. Now all we had to do was find his location so that he could be arrested.

Each day was like putting together a puzzle of new clues to the crazy life that was unfolding before my eyes. It wasn't fun or exciting. It was actually terrible being the center of attention of, "What has Ben done this time?" It was exhausting, to say the least. It was hard to focus on work and be in a good place while raising my daughter, but something great did start to happen while all of this was going on.

Through the trauma, I was developing an amazing relationship with God like I had never known before. I had watched a DVD called *The Secret*, a documentary film where leading scientists, authors, doctors, pastors, and philosophers revealed the 'great secret' that transformed the lives of those willing to live it.[4] The documentary captured me, and I started to adopt the techniques that I learned in the film. I learned how to pray, meditate, and focus on living a happier life. The Lord knew I needed this during this time. It was so transformational for me that I think I shared the DVD with at least eight friends within the first few weeks of owning it.

Around this same time, I had found a non-denominational church that Chelsea Laine and I really loved. So much so, in fact, that we attended church every Sunday. It was a satellite church, so we heard from the Senior Pastor, Ed Young, each week on the big screen. I had never experienced church quite like this before. With every new message I heard, I began to experience life, its struggles and hardships in a whole new way, being moved to tears by a lot of those services.

I began to see God's love and light even though I was facing one of the worst times in my life. It was astonishing to say the least. We met some really nice friends and saw how they interacted with others, which was so refreshing. The praise and worship music, too, was over-the-top amazing. I remember the lead singer was Derric Bonnot, just a kid at the time, most likely 16 or 17. I started to experience "warm fuzzies" while listening to the music. I came to know that this was the way you feel when you are touched by the Holy Spirit. I really felt like we had found our home. Blessings of all kinds were showing up all over my life, which made me better understand that if you draw closer to God, He will draw closer to you!

DISCUSSION QUESTIONS

1. What emotions and thoughts do you imagine Erika was processing while trying to protect her daughter?

2. How did the support of friends, investigators, and family help Erika in this chapter?

3. What would trusting God look like in a season where you feel surrounded by fear or injustice?

Devotional Scripture: Proverbs 18:10 — *The name of the Lord is a fortified tower; the righteous run to it and are safe.*

Reflection: Running isn't always an act of fear—sometimes it's a step toward wisdom and protection.

Prayer: Lord, when I feel surrounded by fear or injustice, help me to run to You first. Remind me that You are my defender and my refuge.

CHAPTER FOURTEEN

WHEN THE PAST FINDS YOU

BACK TO SCHOOL UNDER WATCHFUL EYES

We returned home to Dallas only one day before Chelsea Laine started fourth grade. This was so out of character for me. Typically, I worked her into a school schedule a week before to ease into the school year routine. Still, under the current circumstances, we had no choice. This year, she was starting a new school, Sidney Lanier Expressive Art School, located in downtown Oak Cliff, about a 15-minute drive from her home, where she would be studying dance and theater as well as the normal academics. I chose this school because it seemed to fit her talents, as at the time she was also in the Dallas Symphony Children's Chorus.

When Chelsea Laine started school, I met with the principal and explained all that was going on with her father and that they were under strict orders to not allow Ben into the school. He was not to have any lunchtime visits or be allowed to pick her up from school, ever. We still had no idea of his location.

Not long after she had started school, Chelsea Laine told me that her dad had come by for lunch and brought her out of the school to see his new truck. I was furious that the school did not take me seriously. How could this have slipped through the cracks? What if he would have taken her? I was keeping her from visiting Ben on his weekends because of his lifestyle. As far as I knew, he was homeless, jobless, and back on drugs. We didn't even know where he was living at this time. Another question I had was: *How in the world was he driving a NEW TRUCK?!* He told Chelsea Laine that he had gotten an apartment close to our apartment in downtown Dallas, but didn't say where. That was not comforting at all. Despite being more scared and uncertain than ever, I had to continue acting as normal as I could. Even though I was freaking out on the inside, I tried to act as normal as possible around Chelsea Laine so that I would not alarm her. She didn't understand the big picture of what was going on because she was only ten years old. Instead of freaking out, I responded with, "Oh wow, that's nice. How was your visit?"

She said, "It was fine."

Of course, the first thing I did was contact the school and tell them to please never allow that to happen again. This incident solidified that I urgently needed to do something legally to protect myself and Chelsea Laine, too!

THE PEACE BOND

I met with the Dallas Police Department, and I tried to get a restraining order, with no luck. They simply said with no emotion, "Unless he has already harmed you or threatened you with physical violence, we are unable to file a restraining order on him." *Are you kidding me?*

He was on the run—no one knew where he was living. He was unemployed, using drugs, sending me terrible and threatening voice-mails, and more. I felt helpless being subjected to the ordinances and criteria that were "*the law*." Clearly, something needed to change.

Someone suggested the idea of getting a Peace Bond that would offer some kind of protection. I was willing to do anything to protect myself and Chelsea Laine. A peace bond is an order from a criminal court that requires a person to keep the peace and be on good behavior for a period of time. This essentially means that the person who signs a peace bond must not be charged with any additional criminal offenses during that time. My mom and I went to Grand Prairie, about 20 minutes from where we lived, to meet with a nice judge, and were able to put the peace bond in order on September 3, 2003. I was desperate, and if this was all I could get to feel somewhat protected, then so be it. The best I could hope for was that he would think twice about coming near us.

It started becoming a regular occurrence that I would receive phone calls after phone call from people trying to locate Ben. At this time, we had already been divorced for eight years. One afternoon, I remember receiving a phone call while driving. I answered, "Hello." A woman proceeded to tell me that they were looking for Ben. I asked, "May I ask what for?"

She said, "I am unable to give you that information, but we need to speak to him as soon as possible." Apparently, he had taken out a credit card and was past due on the payment. That would not be the last call of that nature, and I received many more strange calls looking for him.

Tired of living every day with the fear that Ben would show up and do something threatening, we decided to move. Being scared to look over my shoulder or get out of my car, wondering where Ben was living, was just too much for me to handle.

I knew that Ben was out of his mind, and with a history of anger, violence, alcohol, and drug abuse, it wasn't far-fetched that I was afraid he would kill me. Looking back, I truly believe I had developed PTSD. Can you even imagine?

Stop for a minute if you will, close your eyes, and just try to feel what I was feeling. I lived every day afraid for my own life, and worse, the life of my child. It was surreal. I knew or felt in my heart that he would never harm Chelsea Laine. It's something I can't explain.

Meanwhile, I received a phone call from one of Ben's best friends from high school, Roger. They played soccer together and had been buddies for a long time. He asked me if I knew where Ben was.

I said, He is living at his old house in Duncanville." I asked, "Why?"

He said, "Are you home?" I told him I was, and he came over to my apartment carrying a big white envelope with him.

He said, with shock in his eyes, "Ben bought a truck in my name, rented an apartment, and was calling himself, Dr. Davidson!" Pieces of the puzzle started to come together. That's why when I drove over to the apartments where he was arrested and looked through tenant names a week earlier, I hadn't seen his name! That's also how he had a brand-new truck!

Roger planned on going to see Ben the next day. I was a little scared for him, but he insisted. After his visit, Roger and I met up again, and he told me that when he went to visit Ben at his house, he told him that he needed Roger's help! *What nerve!* That's the brain of a drug user, I suppose. I begged and pleaded with Roger to press charges. I needed to feel safe for myself and Chelsea Laine, and felt that this was the only way to do that, and for Ben to sit in jail so he could get sober. Roger pressed charges, and I thought that this would finally change everything. Little did I know, the story was far from over.

One night after visiting with my parents in DeSoto, I was on my way home when I thought, "Maybe I should drive around and see if I see anything." Something my mom had said made me think of our old apartments that we had lived in several years earlier near Deep Ellum. Chelsea Laine was fast asleep in her booster seat, which had a five-point safety buckle. Even though she was ten, she was really little, and I just have a thing for safety.

I still had my remote opener for the apartment complex entrance gate and drove right in. Since we had lived there before, I knew the parking garages very well. There were three of them that were four levels high. I went into the first one, driving very slowly up and down. As I continued, I saw a truck that Chelsea Laine had described to me before, and the truck was driving very slowly. When we passed each other, I realized it was Ben driving the brand-new truck! Panic set in. He sort of stopped, and I slowly kept going. I was trying to get the license plate information, but I was shaking so much that I could hardly write it down. Then he turned his truck around to follow me as I kept going. I was freaking out. He called me, and I didn't answer.

I decided to drive to McKinney Avenue, about five minutes away, where I knew there were a lot of people and it was a very well-lit area. On the drive over, I called the police and explained to them what was going on. My voice was shaking. I pulled over in a drive-through at an upscale lit-up apartment complex and waited for them. Ben had circled by me a few times and must have figured out what I was doing and then left. I was relieved to find him, but still scared. I was so tired and exhausted from all of this going on. I was just ready for his arrest so that I would not have to worry or look over my shoulder anymore. When the police arrived, I told them everything, and they assured me that they would be on the lookout for him.

ARREST NUMBER TWO

The next day, I received a phone call from Ben's father asking if I would be home. This was odd, since we had never had a good relationship, even when Ben and I had been married. I asked what he needed, and he said, "I am going to drop Ben's cat off at your apartment."

I told him, "I already have two cats, and I don't know what you are talking about anyway."

He said, "Did you know that Ben was in jail?"

I said, "No, I didn't."

He then said something disturbing. "Ok, then, if you don't want it, just tell Chelsea Laine that I will go ahead and have the cat put to sleep." I was astonished. I suppose I should have been used to it by now; even during our high school years, my in-laws had always seemed to blame me for their son's wrongdoings, so this was no different.

Later that day, I got a call from the Dallas Police Department telling me that they had found Ben and arrested him around 2 a.m. *Music to my ears!* Now I didn't have to be scared anymore or wonder where he was lurking or if he would show up at Chelsea Laine's school. The anxiety and paranoia were over... At least for a little while, until he was released on bail.

DISCUSSION QUESTIONS

1. Erika faced terrifying uncertainty as she navigated safety concerns for herself and Chelsea Laine. How do you respond when you feel unsafe or powerless? Who or what do you turn to for strength?

2. How did Erika demonstrate courage and resilience, even in the midst of fear, legal limitations, and emotional exhaustion?

3. What does it look like to trust God while still taking active steps to protect yourself and your family?

Devotional Scripture: 2 Thessalonians 3:3 — *But the Lord is faithful, and he will strengthen you and protect you from the evil one.*

Reflection: When the systems around us fall short, God never will. In His faithfulness, He strengthens us, gently directs our steps, and surrounds us with the wisdom, courage, and support we need to carry on. No matter what we face, we are never truly alone—God remains our shield and our deliverer.

Prayer: Lord, thank You for never leaving my side. Even when I feel overwhelmed by fear, help me to trust that You are fighting for me. Strengthen my spirit, guide my steps, and cover me and my loved ones with Your peace and protection. Amen.

CHAPTER FIFTEEN

SHADOWS IN THE SUNLIGHT

LETTERS FROM JAIL

Ben was convicted of stealing the Tahoe and spent eight months in jail. During that time, he began writing letters to Chelsea Laine. I wasn't sure if I should read them before giving them to her, especially considering his poor character and ongoing substance abuse. In the end, I did read them—and then passed them along to her. Most of the letters were filled with him telling her how much he loved her and other stuff that honestly felt meaningless or ridiculous to me at the time. I can't remember everything he wrote, but I do remember thinking they were just filled with empty words.

While Ben was incarcerated, his parents hired an attorney to obtain grandparent rights. If these rights were given, they would be able to have Ben's visitation with Chelsea Laine while he was in jail. This was unbelievable to me! These are the same people who were never supportive in helping us or encouraging us in our relationship, in our marriage, or in being a family. Other than waiting at our house for an appliance, there were very few occasions that were positive or helpful. Now they want visitation rights? The first year after I had left Ben, when Chelsea Laine was only a year old, Ben did not pay any child support for the entire year until our divorce was final. The only reason he paid then was because he was legally obligated. At the time, he was living with his parents. I had just been on the phone with him, asking him for a little financial help. I had just gone to the grocery store and spent $150. He said, "How much do you need?"

I said, "I don't know. I told you I just spent $150 at the grocery store. Maybe $100."

We would have the same conversations over and over for the rest of the year, and Chelsea Laine and I never received a dime. After that conversation, I went over to pick up Chelsea Laine.

He and his mother came out to the car with a grocery sack in each hand. I took them and looked in each bag and said, "No, thank you! I just told Ben that I went to the grocery store. I don't need your charity, I need money!" I was furious! This was another example of how he rarely listened to me or tried to help me. This may seem ungrateful, but I just went to the grocery store and needed money for other expenses.

I learned later during the arbitration in their attorney's office that Ben's parents had hired a private investigator. Apparently, he was following me, trying to get any evidence to prove that I was an unfit mother. *What?! Me, an unfit mother?* I couldn't believe it. Their son was a criminal, a drug user... *And I was unfit?* Ultimately, their private investigator thought that I lived a pretty wild and crazy life, just because we went to live concerts. I lived alone and never had men spend the night. I went to work and church. I took Chelsea Laine to Vacation Bible School, and she went to camp for one week. This was just another indication that I had no support or encouragement from Ben or his family. I was struggling so hard to make a normal life for us, and instead of supporting their grandchild, they spent about $80,000 to get Chelsea Laine taken away from me. All of this while their son sat in jail for theft. It broke my heart that they wouldn't help us. What a sad story for Chelsea Laine's grandparents.

BEN AND HIS LAWYER

Upon reading one of Ben's letters from jail, Chelsea Laine had told me that her dad had a girlfriend. I found that to be pretty strange since he was in jail. It didn't take long before I put two and two together and figured out that Ben's attorney, whom I had met in the arbitration, named Lisa, must have been who she was talking about. Who else could he be dating while he was in jail? I didn't have any proof, but made a note in the back of my mind and also told my attorney, Polly, and my mother of my suspicions. Since Ben had a past of being pretty dishonest, it wouldn't surprise me.

Not long after, I discovered that all of the charges Roger had filed against Ben for stolen identity had miraculously been dropped. *Surely no coincidence*, I thought. We were on our way to court for a pretrial when I got a call from my attorney. "Erika," Polly said.

I said, "Yes?"

"As your attorney, I need to inform you of something. Can you talk?"

"Yes, go on."

Polly continued, "I have to tell you that someone from our office saw Lisa and Ben holding hands after our hearing today."

I felt like I was living in a *Lifetime* movie or a *Dateline* story. My criminal ex-husband was dating his attorney, who was married and had a child! You could have knocked me over with a feather.

It was September 27, 2004, in the District Court 254th Judicial District, Dallas County, Texas. We were finally going to court to modify the Parent-Child Relationship decree that had been set years before. I didn't want Ben anywhere near Chelsea Laine until he was rehabilitated from his addiction and back on his feet.

I went to Polly's office for a meeting before the big trial. I walked into the room and started to panic. The large conference room table was filled with stacks and stacks of files that were all to support my case. The whiteboard was covered with plans and instructions for Polly's strategy for the trial. All that was on my mind was, *Is this all for me?* The weight of the financial burden had set in. When we were reviewing the plan, Polly told me that she let Ben's attorney know that we knew about them dating, and Lisa turned green like she was sick.

I have to admit that I did have thoughts of reporting her for breaking rules by dating her client, but I decided that it was not my place to seek revenge. Even though I was upset, I knew I had to surrender this over to Jesus so that He could fight this battle for me.

I was trying to stay calm, but the fact that my ex-husband was dating his attorney was almost too much to handle emotionally. I walked into the courtroom with my family. We heard whispers and then found out that they were not going to allow my mom or family to sit in the courtroom for the trial, since they might need to call on them as witnesses. They had no actual intentions of doing this—it was just a ploy to make me uncomfortable and feel unstable, and it worked.

I couldn't even stand the appearance of Ben. Going through the trial was really difficult on my own without my family. Little did he or anyone else know that I had about 30 friends and supporters in the courtroom, of whom he didn't know. It was definitely one of the craziest and stressful times I had ever gone through in my life, so it felt good to have all of those supporters. I had lived for the past several years caught in a suffocating web, and I was ready for it to be over.

Then the court proceedings began. I was sitting in my chair, next to Polly, and I found a way to adjust my chair so that I did not have to look at Ben while he was on the stand for questioning. Almost every time Polly would ask him a question, he would bold-faced lie. It was truly unbelievable the way he could sit there with a straight face and continue to lie over and over. I began to lean over so that I could see him clearly and he could see me. Then and only then would he tell the truth, every time. This whole thing was just unbelievable.

Polly was incredible that day in court. She nailed him to the cross, so to speak, which he deserved. I had been tortured for so long, and it was finally his turn. As we got to the end of the closing arguments. Polly, I, Ben's attorney, and Ben were all standing in front of the judge as he was about to make his ruling. He began reading everything we had agreed upon, and I started to feel as if someone had cupped their hands over my ears and everything was muffled.

OVERWHELMED IN COURT

Suddenly, panic set in. My mind was racing through everything Chelsea Laine and I had endured. *What in the world am I doing? Am I agreeing to these terms out of fear? Am I crazy to agree to these terms?* As all of this was rushing through my head, a euphoric feeling came over me. It was as if everything the judge was saying sounded like the teacher in the *Charlie Brown* cartoon. *Wah, wah, wah.* I didn't understand anything the judge was saying. All of a sudden, I burst into tears.

Polly looked over at me and called for a recess. We started to walk to the side of the courtroom through a door to a private room. Polly sat down at the table as I stood. I asked her to please just review everything that we had agreed upon. I asked her, "Am I doing the right thing? What would you do? Would you agree to these terms?"

I remember thinking, *I have to agree to something.* I was already facing $26,000 in attorney fees, so in a way, I felt like I had to just agree and get it over with. Polly looked at me with the most sincere and loving face—like an angel was right before me—and said, "If you do not feel comfortable with this agreement, we can start over."

Tears ran down my face. I felt so much pressure and anxiety. I looked at her and said, "Polly, you've already done so much work and spent so much time on this case, and I owe you $26,000 even as of now."

She said, "I don't care; it doesn't matter. I want you to feel comfortable with everything that you're agreeing to today. The money doesn't matter. We can start over." I had chills down my spine and knew in my heart that she meant every word.

I felt a huge relief, but soon after, I said, "Please just review everything with me again so that I can understand." As she walked me through the agreement, I began to feel somewhat relieved.

According to the new agreement, Ben had to remain clean from drugs and work through five phases in order to return to standard visitation. The five phases were:

1. Supervised visits.
2. Ben must attend weekly counseling sessions for a period of one year.
3. Ben and I attend individual and joint sessions of counseling.
4. The court-ordered counselors had to agree upon Ben's progress to allow him to move forward with unsupervised time with Chelsea Laine.
5. Phase five would grant Ben unsupervised visits, and he would eventually return to his regular standard visitation.

Stair-stepped visitation agreements are a way to incentivize a troubled parent to seek recovery. If the parent follows through with their rehabilitation expectations, then every 30 days or so, the visitation allowance increases.

After she explained the agreement, I felt a sense of relief. I took a deep breath and we walked back into the courtroom and approached the bench with him and his girlfriend's attorney, Lisa. After the judge gave his ruling, we were free to go, but guess what? Ben's parents were held responsible for over $18,000, while I still owed several thousand dollars of my $26,000 bill to Polly. I told her that she could come in and I would do her nails and pedicures until the debt was paid. She said, "You don't owe me anything. Debt cancelled. Now go and begin your life again!" I couldn't believe this! I hugged her, and I'm sure I cried. I was ready for a new beginning.

DISCUSSION QUESTIONS

1. What parts of Erika's legal battle stood out to you as most unjust or painful?

2. How did God show up through people like Polly and others in her support system?

3. What can we learn about perseverance and discernment through Erika's courtroom journey?

Devotional Scripture: Isaiah 41:10 — *So do not fear, for I am with you; do not be dismayed, for I am your God. I will strengthen you and help you; I will uphold you with my righteous right hand.*

Reflection: God does not leave us in the courtroom moments of our lives. He strengthens us through the process and surrounds us with unexpected help.

Prayer: Father, when I face overwhelming odds or unjust situations, be my strength. Give me clarity and courage to keep standing for what is right.

PICTURES

San Francisco KDIA

Ginny & Erika

Chelsea Laine & her
Youth Pastor

Chelsea Laine singing
at Fellowship Church

Chelsea Laine & Livy

Preston& Chandler

Brennan & Sarah
Talia, Mila, & Max

Dylan & Savannah
Wrenley & Hallie

Erika & ShelleyJane

ShelleyGood & Erika

Kay(Erika's Mom)

Chelsea Laine, Livy, Erik,
Billy & Nancy Fields

Cousins

Ann, Chucky, Erika & Karen

Erika, Ann, Karen

Ann, Erika & Karen

Chelsea Laine & Erika

CL, Dior, Bella, & Erika

Erika & Chelsea Laine

Chelsea Laine & Erika

Erika in 7ᵗʰ grade

The Valentine
Coronation

Erika & Shannon the
Mad Hatter

Freshman Therese Bundy
smiles excitedly as she is announced Class Favorite.
(Photo by Michael Jackson.)

Senior Chris Martin con-
gratulates senior Erika Sea-
meyer as she is chosen Class
Favorite.

Chris Martin & Erika
1987

Danielle &
Chelsea Laine

Tyler & Chelsea Laine

Chelsea Laine& Tyler

Chelsea Laine
& Stephanie

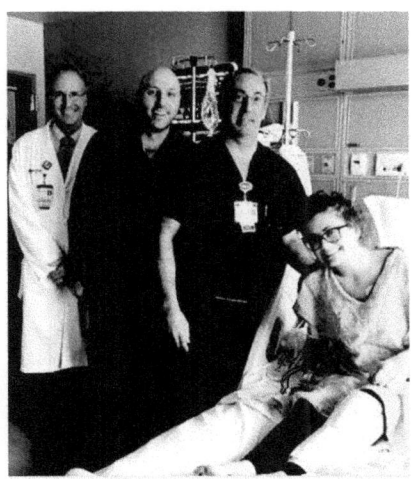

UT Southwestern Neurology~
Dr.White, Dr.Pride, & Dr.Fiesta

Chelsea Laine's new car
after brain surgery

CL, Michelle, Randy, Donna
& me Nashville, TN

Yuki,Erika,Tammy & Erik

Nana & Chelsea Laine,
Erika at Graceland

Chelsea Laine & Erika

Renewing our
wedding vows

Erik & Erika at Deer
Mountain Village, SD

Eric, Raquelle, Erik & Erika

Earnestine, Erika &
Chelsea Laine

Some of my BFF's
Amazing Grace Retreats

Inaugural Amazing
Grace Retreats

Jay & Paige

Niece Lyndsey & Erika

Paige and Erika

Paige and Lyndsey

Family

Daddy & Erika

Erika, Ann & Karen

Mama & Daddy at
Fellowship Church

Chelsea Laine & her
brother

Sam, & Sonya the OG
South Dakota Sisters

Angel Faces

Chelsea Laine singing
at Fellowship Church

Erik & Erika

Erik, Cindy, Dave & Erika

Belinda & Erika

Tish & Erika

Kim Clab & Erika

Texas & South Dakota

TCD Shot Girls at
Cooper Tennis

Erika & Pastor Becky

Stephen & Erika

Mimi & Livy

JODI LARUE PHOTOGRAPHY

Chelsea Laine &
Stephanie

Chelsea Laine &
Niece Lyndsey

BFF Corky & Erika

Erik, Erika, Chelsea Laine & Nick

Robin my side kick aka Sissa & Erika

Erik, Rosalie & Erika at Trinity Church

Beverly & Erika

The Big house

The Olan Mills Seamayer
family potrait

Karen, Ann & Erika

Chelsea Laine &
Cydney Ann

Rachee & Chelsea Laine

Nicole, Mama Jo, Raquelle, Monique, & Erika

Chelsea Laine,Jenny & Erika~Isla Mujeres, Mexico

Pastor Kay Pulley (my cousin) & Sisters

Erika, Nonie, Madalyn, Chelsea Laine

Carolyn & Erika

BFF Becky, & Erika

Robert & Erika

Heidi & Erika

Wedding in Cozumel,
Mexico

Nico, Chelsea Laine,
Natalia & Erika

Erika, ShelleyJane &
Ginger

Tennis Team in 7ᵗʰ Grade at Byrd Jr. High

Sturgis Rally 2016

Chelsea Laine & Dior

Dawn & Erika

Chelsea Laine's
Graduation at Black Hills
State University

Erika & Jeremy aka
Foxy Arms

Best Guy Friends

Amazing Grace Ministries
Golf Tournament 2025

Randy Melancon &
Erika

Chelsea Laine & Aeriel

Chelsea Laine, Lynette
& Erika

Ursula, Chelsea
Laine, Monique, Aeriel

Kirsten, Tracy & Erika

Childhood Best
Girlfriends

Family

Bella, niece Alex, Chelsea
Laine & nephew Nicholas

Shan Stan & Erika

Chelsea Laine & Mimi

Dantia & Erika

Erika, Jay,
Chelsea Laine

Singer/Songwriter
Dante Bowe & Erika

Chelsea Laine & Paige

Chelsea Laine &
Lyndsey

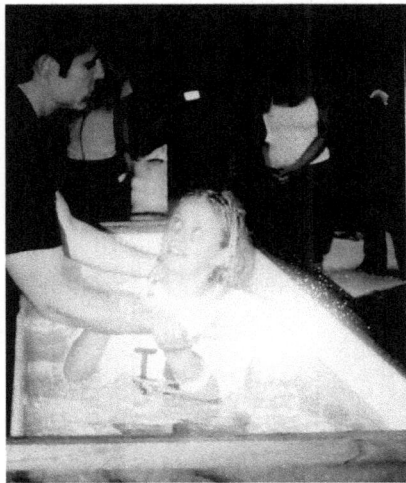

Chelsea Laine Baptism

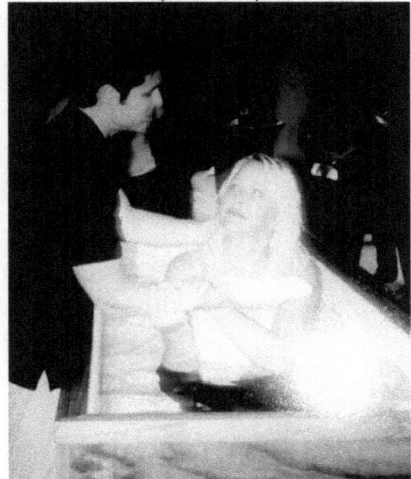

Erika's Baptism

Darlene, Erika &
Chelsea Laine~1994

Erika, Eric & Bobby

Lisa, Erika's publisher
& friend

Daddy, Erika, Karen &
Ann on Falling Leaves

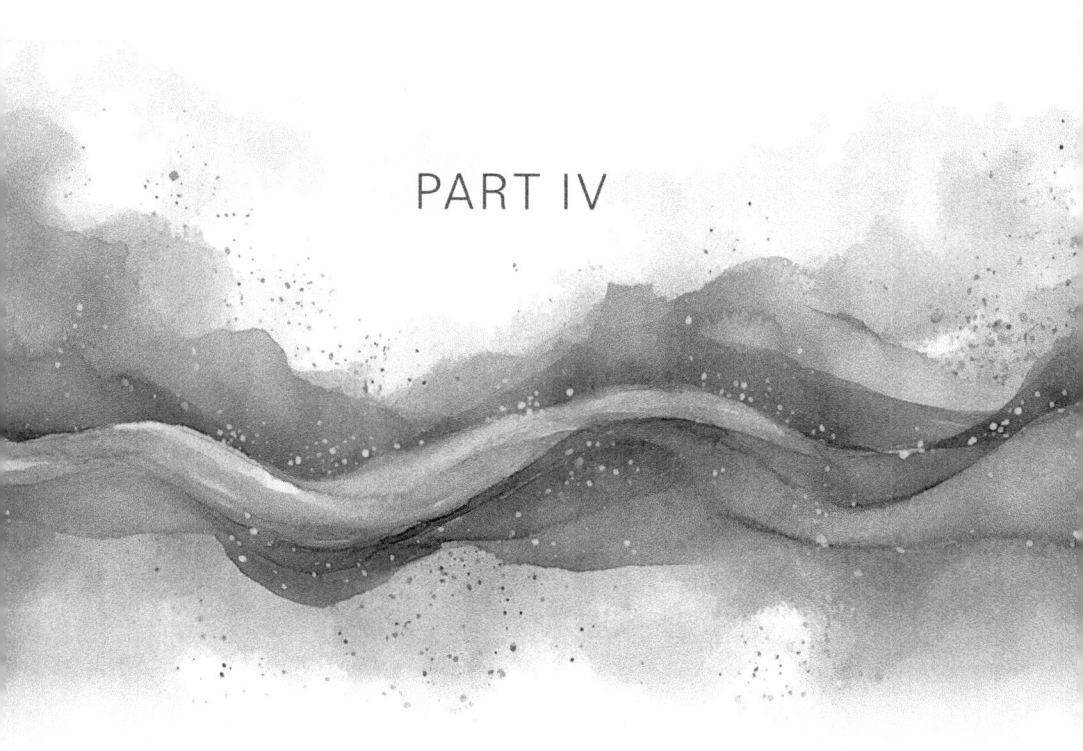

PART IV

HEALING TO WHOLENESS

CHAPTER SIXTEEN

FRESH AIR AND FORWARD STEPS

A SAFE HAVEN

And so, the rebuilding of our life began. We moved into Highland Park on Abbott Avenue. For those of you who don't live in Dallas, Highland Park and Park Cities are like the Beverly Hills of California. The quiet streets were adorned with lavish homes, mature trees, and nannies walking their clients in baby strollers that cost as much as a car. It was a peaceful, beautiful place to call home. Best of all, it was in the Highland Park school district, one of the best in the area. The locals call it "the bubble," and it is called that for good reason. The neighborhood is like something you would see in a movie set. It is a very safe community, with a lot of stay-at-home moms wearing one of two things: high-end workout clothes or designer clothing.

Highland Park Village was home to many couture shops such as Ralph Lauren, Cartier, Dior, Fendi, Hermes, and Chanel. There were also great restaurants like Cafe Pacific, Mi Cocina, and Bird Bakery. There was a lightness in the air, and carefree people sipping their afternoon Starbucks pick-me-ups with a friend was a common sight. From Thanksgiving to Christmas, the trees were filled with twinkling lights, and horse-drawn carriages took patrons on rides through lavish communities decorated for the season.

The Katy Trail was being built directly behind our apartments, which ran through the Uptown and Oak Lawn areas of Dallas. It followed the former rail bed of the Missouri-Kansas-Texas Railroad, previously known as the MKT Road. The Katy Tennis Courts and a playground were only a block away.

I was grateful to have found a nice three-bedroom, two-bath apartment in Highland Park in which to start the next chapter of our lives. The apartments that we had lived in up until now were brand new and modern. This apartment had a different vibe all on its own. The style was a little outdated, but I loved the neighborhood and schools so much that it was worth the sacrifice. Instead of being in the Downtown Dallas area, we were now in an established, beautiful neighborhood just three miles or less away from our old apartments. Moving there was one of the best decisions I ever made.

One of the reasons for moving was for security and peace of mind. I had found out that it takes a while to receive an active response from the Dallas Police Department. But Highland Park had their own police department servicing a small five-mile radius. It felt a little bit like Mayberry; if you called, the police could be at your house in two to five minutes or less. It was exactly the comfort I needed.

As an added bonus, the manager of the apartments lived directly across from our apartment and owned a gun. Everybody knew everybody, and several of my neighbors knew my story and situation. We were taken under their wings, and our neighbors were quite protective of us. It truly was a blessing to live in such a great community following such a traumatic time. I was really grateful to have been able to move to such a nice area.

The public schools in the Highland Park neighborhood operated more like private schools and were quite strict. The school district, as I mentioned before, was highly sought after for many reasons. Chelsea Laine was struggling a bit to understand some of her work, so I had her tested by the diagnostician, and they discovered that she was a visual and tactile learner. One of the best things that happened for Chelsea Laine was that she had a co-teacher in her math and reading class. She was also able to take tests in another room or have the questions for a test read to her, rather than her having to read them. The cool thing was that the other students probably just thought they were "teacher's aïds" and helped Chelsea Laine (and a few other students who had similar learning styles), and she never felt singled out. This was a stark contrast to my experience at her age, when I was put into the special education classroom upon discovering I was a visual-tactile learner. This program at Highland Park was a total game-changer for Chelsea Laine, and it made my mama's heart so proud to see her grow and flourish in this environment.

A NUDGE TO LISTEN

Life was pretty quiet and normal for about a year or so. I allowed Chelsea Laine to go over to visit Ben even when it was outside of his regular visitation time. Why would I do this, you may be thinking? Well, it's simple. When I felt a nudge from God to do things that would normally be out of the ordinary, I chose to be obedient, and later, I believe it served us well. To some of you who may be non-believers or new to your Christian walk, you may call this common sense. I will tell you that I was led by the Holy Spirit to allow these things, putting my faith in God first and leaning on His understanding, rather than my own, just like the Scripture says:

Trust in the Lord with all your heart, and lean not on your own understanding. In all your ways acknowledge him, and he will direct your steps (Proverbs 3:5-6 NIV).

Had I only relied on my own thoughts, I would never have allowed her to go. October rolled around, and Chelsea Laine asked me if she could go trick-or-treating with Lisa, and Lisa's daughter, Hailey. Hailey lived primarily with her father, but spent weekends with her mom, and she and Chelsea Laine had really hit it off. At first, her request made me a little sad. Why would she want to go with him instead of being with me? But I had to remember that all of the adult issues I experienced were not hers. For her, she was just a little girl who longed for her daddy's affection and attention. Letting go and reminding myself of this truth was one of the hardest things to do. However, I firmly believed and still do that it is incredibly important to separate your feelings from your children's. I spent a lot of time with Jesus, talking to Him like a friend. I prayed a lot for peace and comfort. After I prayed, I got that nudge from God, and I felt in my spirit the peace to allow Chelsea Laine to go trick-or-treating with her father, Lisa, and Hailey.

After years of hurt, neglect, abuse, fear, anguish, and disappointment with Ben, you can only imagine how difficult it was for me to willingly hand over my precious and innocent little girl to her "Daddy," who had been such a monster to me.

Looking back on my life, God has always given me a supernatural ability for discernment when needed. As I grew in my walk with Jesus and trusted in my faith more seriously, I would choose to be obedient to his voice and little nudges along the way. It always worked out for the best in the long run.

As time went on, Lisa became increasingly rude and mean towards Chelsea Laine. By this time, Chelsea Laine had her own cell phone,

Lisa would constantly text her, nitpicking on little things or pestering her about her grades in school, making Chelsea Laine a nervous wreck. I felt so sad for Chelsea Laine and hated to see what it did to her little soul. Chelsea Laine was such a loving, happy child with an optimistic attitude. She was always thinking of others and tried her best to please Lisa. Unfortunately, Lisa didn't have Chelsea Laine's best interests at heart, and slowly, I saw the joy drain out of her.

Sometimes on the weekends Chelsea Laine spent with them, they would take Hailey to horseback riding lessons. Chelsea Laine loved horses and had ridden many times in her life and taken lessons too, but was never asked if she would like to participate in taking lessons with Hailey. Instead, she just had to tag along, sit there, and watch. I truly believe Lisa was trying to punish me by hurting Chelsea Laine.

On February 21, 2007 (Chelsea Laine was 13 years old), Lisa and Ben had their first child together, a baby boy named Hayes, who had Down Syndrome. They purchased Ben's childhood home from his parents, which put them about 20 minutes from our apartment. One afternoon, I drove out to pick up Chelsea Laine from her weekend with them. I normally called her ahead of time and told her to meet me outside so that I could just pick her up and be on our way quickly; because Ben, Lisa, and I had no relationship whatsoever, and I didn't want to risk either of them coming outside to talk. But for some reason on this particular afternoon, I felt a nudge from God again. I didn't understand it at the time, but I chose to listen, be obedient, and follow what I heard and felt in my heart.

When Chelsea Laine came outside, I noticed it was a particularly beautiful day. There were a lot of trees in their front yard, and the sun was warm and soft. I said, "Chelsea Laine, go inside and get your little brother. I want to take a pic of y'all!" He was just a baby, maybe eight months old, and she was 13 years old. She went into the house and brought him outside, holding him on her hip. I took a picture of the two of them. It was a beautiful picture, and after the next chapter, you will understand why it was one of the most special pictures of the two of them ever taken.

One afternoon, I was talking with one of my girlfriends about my struggles with our situation with Ben and his wife, and she mentioned something I hadn't thought of before. She reminded me that in the past, when Ben seemed like he was causing unnecessary problems, typically, he was hiding something. I thought about what she said, and it all made sense. We decided to look his name up on a public data website out of curiosity, and sure enough, there was something new on his record! It said that he had been arrested, but it did not indicate what the charges were.

In order to find out, I had to go personally to the Lew Sterrett Justice Center and pay a fee to pull up the full record. I can still remember exactly how I felt and what I was wearing that day. It was almost as if the anxiety I was feeling put me in a state of mind that felt like a temporary coma. My body slouched in the chair as I stared at the floor, and my mind shut down for 15 minutes while I was waiting for the report. I felt numb, waiting for that report, already dreading the emotional torment I would be facing, opening up the can of worms that was Ben's unsavory life once again.

When the social worker called my name, I walked sheepishly to the counter. They handed the police report to me, and although I was scared of what I might read in the report, I couldn't read it fast enough. As I got about halfway down the page, it stated that Ben had thrown a drink in someone's face at a piano bar somewhere in Dallas, and he was arrested for evading arrest. As I read those words, I shouted out, *"YES!"* as if I were at a football game watching the Cowboys score a touchdown. I got chills all over my body, and I said out loud, *"I'm free!* I'm FREE!" As tears filled my eyes and started to fall down my face, I felt the most exhilarating feeling come over me, knowing that because of this news, Chelsea Laine and I wouldn't have to put up with Ben and Lisa's bullying, hatred, or manipulation any longer.

Because our last court document stated that if he were to get in any kind of trouble whatsoever with the law, he was supposed to notify me (and of course, he didn't), then it was a breach of agreement for him to have hidden this arrest from me. As I was walking out of the building, I called my attorney to tell her the news of his arrest. We immediately put together an email stating that I was aware of his arrest and that it would be in his best interest to be on his best behavior from here on out. I had hoped this would put an end to the harassment, and he and Lisa would magically be on their best behavior. That was not the case. Instead, I ended up with an unimaginable reply from Ben, written by Lisa. The email simply reads, *Do not contact me by email, by phone, or by letter.*

In all that we had gone through, even with his addiction, I knew one thing was true: Ben loved his daughter. It simply wasn't his first choice to relinquish his parental rights, but it seemed to be Lisa's plan all along—get rid of Chelsea Laine and me, once and for all.

For years, Chelsea Laine and I had been riddled with so much pain and embarrassment from all of the interactions and bad decisions put on us by her father. So many times, people would say things to me like, "This just doesn't happen to people." It had been over five years of ups and downs, ins and outs of a rollercoaster ride because of him. It was emotionally, financially, and spiritually challenging, to say the least. To this day, I can't tell you what it meant to both of us to have a strong relationship with the Lord and to have the support of our church family.

Though I felt well cared for and protected by so many, it was more than I could handle being the constant center of attention for all of Ben's wrongdoings. Oftentimes, I would daydream about running away to a land far, far away... To a land where people didn't know us as "poor Chelsea Laine and Erika." I longed to live in a place where I didn't have to feel afraid. Although all of them meant well, it was tiresome, and I didn't want to feel as if I was a victim for the rest of my life. There was a short period of time during which I was grateful for a good friend telling me I had the right to feel like a victim—because I was a victim—but part of my healing was realizing that it didn't have to be my eternal identity. Because of Jesus, I knew that I had a new identity in Christ, and that carried me through my healing and into the next chapter.

THE FINAL GOODBYE

I searched for the right words to say to my daughter as I carefully explained to her that, as far as I could tell, she wouldn't see her father, Lisa, Hailey, or Hayes ever again. We held each other and cried. As tears washed over our faces, thinking of the sheer feeling of abandonment my sweet girl was experiencing, I called on God for His help to know what to say to comfort her. "Chelsea Laine," I said. "For now, you will have to lean on God to be your father until He finds you a sufficient one. He will give you strength and show you His love and fulfill you. This is all you will ever need."

These Scriptures were a comfort to us during this time:

He heals the brokenhearted and binds up their wounds (Psalm 147:3 NIV). This verse highlights God's compassion and ability to mend emotional and spiritual pain, offering comfort and restoration.[5]

He gives power to the faint; and to them that have no might he increases strength (Isaiah 40:29 NIV). This verse emphasizes God's ability to empower and strengthen those who are weary and lack power.

The next day, the school called and told me that they had a bag in the office that Chelsea Laine's dad had left for her. The people in the office had no idea what was going on. I'm sure they thought it was just a normal thing between divorced parents. Little did they know that what was in this bag was the end of a father/daughter relationship! Apparently, it had some of her belongings that her dad and stepmom thought she would want. I thanked the lady in the office, took the bag, and drove home. My emotions were all over the place, realizing that this was the end of their relationship as she knew it. There was a part of me that felt relieved, but I also felt great sorrow for my daughter for losing a relationship with the only father she had ever known.

As I carried the bag inside our apartment, my anxiety and feelings of anger began to build higher and higher. My stomach was in knots, and I was close to tears, but I tried to stay strong as I had for the past five years of this nonsense. *Surely, he had left a note*, I thought. As I looked inside the bag and started opening up zippers and feeling inside the pockets of the bag, I found nothing other than a few clothing items and a stuffed animal. I began to cry frantically. How could this be happening? How was I going to tell Chelsea Laine that her father didn't even leave a note? What an empty feeling to not be able to collect all of your belongings and say goodbye to your dad and his family one last time. It was unbearable. The sadness wept through my body for the reality that she was facing and the pain that she would have to endure.

Chelsea Laine was a gift from God, and it crushed me that she was about to experience the feeling of true abandonment by the one person who was supposed to be her source of safety and stability. All I could do was reflect on my childhood, thankful that I never had to experience any of these emotions or feelings growing up. Not once had I ever thought my parents didn't love me, or experienced them lying to me, or abandoning me. I always *knew* they were there for me, even if we didn't see eye to eye.

In the still of my sadness, I still had an overwhelming sense of hope. *We are free!* I began searching on Craigslist for a way out. I was searching for a new beginning, for a fresh start. I had no idea what I was looking for; I just knew that I wanted to be anywhere but Dallas, even though it was the only home we had ever known. I wanted to be far, far away, where we could feel safe in a place where I didn't have to talk about what had happened. I wanted a fresh start where we could meet new friends with smiles on our faces and love in our hearts. I had been trapped in survival mode for so long that I began to lose sight of who I truly was. I was ready for an adventure.

Looking back, I never could have imagined what was coming next.

DISCUSSION QUESTIONS:

1. Have you ever had to let go of something painful to make space for healing? What helped you take that step?

2. How has God used others—like a friend, mentor, or stranger—to encourage you at just the right time?

3. What does trusting God with your "next step" look like in your life today?

Devotion Scripture: Isaiah 30:21— *Whether you turn to the right or to the left, your ears will hear a voice behind you, saying, 'This is the way; walk in it.*

Reflection: Letting go doesn't always mean forgetting—it often means healing. When you trust God with your pain, He not only carries the burden but gently leads you into peace and restoration. The step forward might be unknown, but it's never unguided when you're walking with Him.

Prayer: God, thank You for being near in the seasons of heartbreak and healing. Help me to let go of what has wounded me so I can step into the future You've prepared. Guide my steps with peace and surround me with Your love. Amen.

CHAPTER SEVENTEEN

A NEW LIFE IN THE HAMPTONS

A LEAP TOWARD A NEW BEGINNING

As I began to look for jobs on Craigslist, I asked myself, "What would I like to do?" I liked horses and playing tennis, and I just wanted to break out of the mold of everything that I had known. I needed a fresh start to find my true self again without all of the worry, stress, and anxiety that had been riddling my life for so long. I loved New York and had been there many times for various events with my friends' band. With that in mind, I began looking for jobs in the Hamptons on Long Island, New York. It must have been another nudge from God. I soon found a nanny job in East Quogue. The ad stated that the mother was a writer, had twin boys, and needed a nanny. She had a big house where I could live rent-free while working—and it gave me the chance to get out of Dallas!

Because of the bad child support check that Ben had given me years ago from an account that didn't exist, my credit had been ruined, and therefore I had no credit card to fall back on and surely no savings. I scrounged up enough money for the trip and booked my flight. I rented a car and drove to her house. It was an amazing house. The boys were sweet, and I got to meet their current nanny, who was leaving due to health issues. I was offered the job on the spot! I was so excited for a new start in a faraway place where nobody would know our terrible past and everything we had been through. We were finally going to be able to live the life that we chose on our terms. I wanted to arrive about two weeks before Christmas so Chelsea Laine and I could enjoy the city's holiday festivities before I started working.

I had also secured a job teaching tennis in East Hampton at the Tennis Club, but that was not starting until the summer—another nudge from God.

During this time, I began to date a guy named Noah. Even though I had already committed to moving to NY, we still continued to date. He was much younger than me, but was such a sweetheart, and this was so special to me after the loveless, hurtful, and painful relationship with Ben. Noah and I had great conversations, and we really liked each other. I believe he was placed in my life for many reasons.

For one, he had been homeschooled and had an amazing relationship with his brothers and his parents. He had been raised with a strong relationship with God. One evening, he invited me over to have dinner with his family, which was lovely. If we were closer in age or had met at another time in our lives, maybe things would have worked out, but I think God had a bigger purpose for this relationship. Packing and putting most of your worldly possessions into storage and moving to another state is a lot of work, and Noah was right there by my side to offer his support. It's like he was some kind of angel sent to help me and also to show me that there were men out there who were respectable, loving, and kind.

I flew back home and began to pack and get rid of as much stuff as I could. I'm sure my friends were thinking, *Has she lost her mind?* My mom was beside herself that we were leaving right before Christmas, but this was one time I had to think about Chelsea Laine and me. I had to leave as quickly as possible. I felt as though I would explode if I stayed in Dallas any longer. You may be wondering how Chelsea Laine was feeling. I believe she was ready for a new chapter, too! Moving away was our chance to have a fresh start, and she was ready.

We packed up as much stuff as the Jeep would hold and said our goodbyes. Noah drove to New York with Chelsea Laine and me, which was such a nice and caring thing to do. He made sure that we made it safely to our destination, which took a couple of days. When we arrived, he helped us get settled into our rooms, and then we drove Noah to New York to do some sightseeing before going to the airport. We knew our relationship wasn't sustainable long-distance, so we parted ways with a bittersweet goodbye. I was so grateful that he was there to help and support us on this journey.

AN UNEXPECTED TURN

We had a nice time over the Christmas break with my new boss, Sarah, and her family. Sarah made us feel very welcome, giving us presents on Christmas morning. Yes, it was different spending the holiday with practical strangers, but we were having fun.

It wasn't long before I started to notice strange things. First of all, she was no writer, and she wanted me to watch her twins 24/7. There were just a couple of fishy things going on. Nothing danger-ous or anything like that, but I felt that it was just not a good fit. She and I had already agreed that I would work certain hours and then be off to work at another job. During the holiday break, Chelsea Laine and I ventured out to nearby towns and discovered a beautiful town called Sag Harbor. Sag Harbor is a coastal village tucked away on the eastern tip of Long Island. It is really beautiful. Little boutiques, art galleries, antique shops, and restaurants where you could grab a bite to eat by the water. It's the kind of place that makes you slow down, breathe, and truly soak it all in.

The view of the beach made it the perfect place for me! I noticed a cute salon at the end of the village by the water, so I went in and asked if they were hiring. I had been a nail technician, makeup artist, medical aesthetician, permanent makeup artist, and instructor for over 15 years. They said they were hiring, and I was so excited.

While working at this salon, I met some really nice people. One of the nail technicians, named Dorota, was a beautiful blonde originally from Poland. Also working there was Sean, who was an amazing hairstylist. Andrea, an esthetician, and I really hit it off. The owners of the salon owned a house a few miles away from the salon, surrounded by big, tall, beautiful trees. This house had been a home for many of the stylists who worked at the salon. During the summer touristy months, there wasn't any affordable housing, so this was a solution for their employees. Pretty cool, if you ask me! And guess what? They offered a room to live in if I wanted to work there!

I had only worked as a nanny for maybe three weeks, but I could already tell that watching the twins all day and all night with no break was not going to work for me. This was my chance to leave the nanny job, so I did! I just told my boss that school was starting back up, and I really wanted Chelsea Laine to go to school in Sag Harbor. It worked and I didn't feel bad at all. I quickly went to the middle school in Sag Harbor and secured a place for Chelsea Laine, and we packed up and left!

FINDING FREEDOM IN SAG HARBOR

Even though it was just a bedroom, we made it our home, and all of the people we lived and worked with were so nice. Sean, the hair stylist, was just across the hall upstairs from Chelsea Laine and me. He was originally from Trinidad and Tobago with a beautiful accent. He was so nice and sometimes stopped by our room to visit and play Bratz dolls with Chelsea Laine! There were lots of laughs. It was so much fun. We simply felt free to be just us with no worry or stress of Ben or Lisa lurking around.

Chelsea Laine and I had never experienced a climate this cold, so we didn't have adequate winter clothing, and I didn't know a thing about layering, being from Texas. I remember Dorota giving me a warm coat as a gift, and that really touched me! This was such a sweet and kind gesture.

As Chelsea Laine and I were exploring one night, we decided to drive out on the beach in our rear-wheel drive Jeep. Up until this point, living in a city, I knew nothing of a 4x4 or the power it had. When we got back into our Jeep to leave, our wheels were just spinning and spinning in the sand, and quickly, we were stuck. I was so embarrassed and felt so dumb not to have known better. I called Dorota, and she immediately called her friend, who had a Jeep Wrangler 4x4 with a winch on it, and she came to our rescue! As dumb as I felt, it turned out to be a great night! She was friends with a chef, and they invited us over for an amazing dinner with six of their friends. I felt very blessed.

I began looking for a church to attend. I soon found out that what we were used to at our non-denominational church in Dallas was non-existent in this area. I found a Baptist church in a town about 30 minutes away. I really liked the preacher and began to invite my friends to attend with us. I was used to inviting people to church, so this was just normal for me. I know that I planted a seed in at least one person's heart because years later, our friend and roommate Sean told me that when he listened to the song *Indescribable* by Chris Tomlin, it reminded him of me. Isn't that great? We never know what might stick when we follow promptings to say or share with others. I hope that even today, when he hears this song, he understands how much God loves him. That is all we are responsible for in this life: sharing God's love and encouraging others, planting a seed of hope in their lives and hearts!

REBUILDING IN PEACE

Chelsea Laine was in eighth grade and really liked her new school, teachers, and friends. I remember some of my most peaceful times of living there were driving her to school. The road curved through beautiful trees, then led us into the village of Sag Harbor and along the beach. I had grown up going to the Caribbean, where the water was blue and the sun was hot. I had never experienced a winter beach, where beautiful rocks are found in some areas and waves splash against them. Sometimes we would stop at the small and quaint coffee shops that looked like something out of a movie to pick up breakfast for us (not often because we didn't have much money).

After dropping her off, if I didn't have an appointment right away, I would go for a walk along the beach with our little dog Bella, a little black and white Parti-Pomeranian. Bella was so funny and loved running on the beach. I hardly ever had her on a leash because she was trained well, but the beach and waves just jazzed her up so much that sometimes I couldn't get her to get in the car when it was time to go. I would find a crab claw or something like that and wave it over her head and say, "Come here, Bella!" and would catch her so we could go home. These walks were some of the most healing of my journey. I remember a neighborhood that I walked in near the ocean. I noticed a cherry blossom tree that had stood bare in the winter, then burst into bloom, and eventually the petals fell to the ground. As I went on my prayer walks, this tree became a symbol of healing for me.

I have always been an avid walker, so at least four or five days a week, I would walk/run for exercise. These meaningful times gave me many opportunities to pray, think, and simply try to rebuild my personal life that had been stripped away from me because of court battles, trauma, pain, and suffering. Even though I missed my family and friends back in Texas, the freedom and safety I felt outweighed it all. Since Ben had completely relinquished his rights as a father, I was free from having to tell him where we were living. I had been bound by so much that my vision was cloudy, in a sense. But with much prayer and by asking for God's help, I began to find myself again!

During this time, I continued to be the best mom I knew how to be. That meant always putting Chelsea Laine first in everything I did. Since she had been singing in a youth group at Fellowship Church (our home church), I was pleased when she told me that she was asked by her friend at school to sing at their Catholic church along-side her during their contemporary service. I was glad to see her stay involved, not only attending church as we did but serving the way she had been doing since she was in fifth grade.

We met a lot of wonderful people in Sag Harbor. One of them was the owner of a pizza place in town. He was so kind to us and offered Chelsea Laine to come up after school and make her own pizza from time to time. That was so much fun for her! Even though there were a lot of changes that year for her, we just always found a way to be open to new experiences and have fun! I soon wanted to find a place of our own. I saw a sign in a yard near where I was living and called the phone number. I spoke with the lady, and we worked it out that we could move in right away.

During this time, I met a cute guy whom I saw at the Corner Bar in Sag Harbor. He was talking with friends when I noticed him. He reminded me of the way Rob Lowe looked in *About Last Night* with the ball cap on, one of my all-time favorite movies. I noticed him noticing me, and I was noticing him. I went over to talk to him. We flirted for a bit, then walked on the streets of the charming town. We got to know each other better and became friends.

He was kind enough to let Chelsea Laine and me use his washer and dryer since we didn't have one at this time. He was really nice, and his sense of humor was just what I needed at the time. I'd call him Tug Boat Tom. At his job, he would work one week on and one week off. He was not a dog person, so when we would bring Bella with us (as we always did), he would say, "Bella, go play in traffic." This always made Chelsea Laine and me laugh because we knew he was just kidding, and the even funnier thing was, there is NO traffic in the winter in the Hamptons! He even began to teach Chelsea Laine how to play guitar. It was a really fun friendship.

One of the last places we lived was a basement apartment in the area. It was a walkout apartment with a beautiful backyard as our view. It had a kitchenette and one big room with a wood-burning fireplace. It was fully furnished, and we made a makeshift room for Chelsea Laine so that she could have her own space. We were having a great time, but my mom was worried sick about us and had it in her mind that things were terrible. After we had been living in New York for a few months, she flew up to visit us. We showed her around and took her to all of the cool spots we had learned about. My mom is a public speaker, among other things, and always tells the story of how worried she was for us during this time. Ultimately, though, when she came up to visit and asked Chelsea Laine if she was ok not having her own room and stuff like that, she replied, "Mimi, I am having so much fun!" "Look, we put up this sheet to divide my room." It was a cute and cozy spot.

Money was tight and times were tough, but the tradeoff was worth it so that we were able to live in a peaceful, beautiful place far away from the pain and suffering we had known for so many years.

DREAMS REKINDLED

In 2008, I met one of my neighbors who was an amazing photographer. I told her about my idea of opening a studio to shoot high-end style photos. The idea first came to me in high school. It continued to evolve as I delved into the world of being a makeup artist and esthetician. My dream was to open Tyler Laine Studios, a luxury portrait experience complete with spa services, professional hair and makeup, custom wardrobing, and at the end, deliver an heirloom-quality photo album of portraits to my client.

That vision had been growing in me for years. Back in Dallas, I had worked with my friend JD Cantu, an amazingly creative photographer who completely understood my outside-the-box approach. He hired me for many freelance shoots as a makeup artist, and we've stayed good friends to this day—now you can find him shooting on the beaches of Destin, Florida. When I worked at the Spa of Tuscany in Highland Park, the owner let me turn part of the skin studio into *Tyler Laine Studio*. I was so grateful for the people who believed in me, even though that first version of my company never took off. Still, stepping away from the drama and chaos had allowed me to remember my dreams and feel free to chase them again.

Around this time, I met a couple of sweet older ladies who owned a beautiful vintage clothing shop in Bridgehampton. As we talked, they told me about a big warehouse where they stored their overflow of vintage clothing and a photography studio. That's how

I met Andrea, a set designer in New York and part-owner of the studio. Soon after, she invited me to see the space, and it was like a dream! The makeup area had a cool mosaic eye, and the design elements fit my vision for Tyler Laine Studios perfectly. Even though she had previously rented the space to large, well-known companies for thousands of dollars a day, she offered it to me—totally for free! Can you even believe it? I couldn't! It felt like God was giving me another chance.

Of course, I accepted, and we got right to work. I scheduled a couple of photo sessions with my connections, using several of my friends and Chelsea Laine as my models. My oldest sister, Ann, lived in Long Island, about an hour and a half away, and since she was a makeup artist, I asked her to come over and work with me. Together, we created some really cool, magazine-like photographs.

I was having blessings all around… Except for monetary blessings. Despite all of the hard work I was putting into Tyler Laine Studios, it just never took off and ran the way I had hoped. I wondered if the closed doors were for a reason. I remember telling somebody very close to me about what I was doing, and they replied, "Erika, when are you going to let that go?"

I remember feeling so deflated, and it completely killed my drive for the idea. In the end, I totally let it go. A lesson learned: Be careful who you share your biggest dreams with and listen to, even if it is someone you love, because they may just keep you from your destiny. You never know their motives for the advice they are giving you. It could even be out of jealousy or their own fears. Instead, tell God everything, and you will have God's peace, which is far more wonderful than the human mind can understand. Seek what God says about the important things in our lives, your ideas, and dreams. Not people. *His peace will quiet your thoughts and heart in Christ Jesus* (Philippians 4:6-8 NIV).

I believe if you pray and ask for God's direction and walk in obedience, He will give you the desires of your heart. Even though it didn't work out, the shoots we created and the experience of working in that environment filled my soul in a way that was so needed.

PROVISION AND CLOSED DOORS

Business was slow at the salon, so I also worked at another salon in East Hampton to pick up extra clients. I remember one day they had asked me to come over for a few appointments, but I didn't even have enough money to drive there. It was 2008, and in the midst of the worst recession in recent decades. It would have been so helpful if I had a credit card to save me during these tough times, but I didn't. I drove up to a little gas station with my pride left behind and asked this cute little old man if he could put five dollars in my gas tank. I was so embarrassed, but had no other choice. I told him that if he did that, I would come back later that day to pay him back. After working that day at the East Hampton Salon, I immediately went and made good on my word.

Other odd jobs popped up here and there, and I took any opportunity that I came across to use my talents to help Chelsea Laine and me gain some financial traction. One of these was a connection from my friend from Dallas, who was living in Williamsburg, who arranged for me to be a makeup artist for half a day in New York City for a Tiffany & Co. magazine shoot. I packed up my makeup kit and took the train into NYC. The makeup was for a man, which just meant basic grooming and making sure his skin wasn't shiny for the photoshoot. This was probably the easiest makeup job I had ever done. I got paid $750 for half a day, which was equivalent to four hours of work, but they only ended up needing me for about an hour and a half. I was so very grateful for a fun opportunity to make a quick income. This was just one of the many monetary prayers I saw God answer in my life!

Another idea we had for extra income was to have Chelsea Laine audition at a Talent Agency in New York. She had been singing most of her life, modeling, and had done a few acting jobs. We had fun going to the audition, but there were no open doors.

With my permanent makeup business, I charged $500 to $600 for my treatments, but the doors were closed there, too! I just couldn't understand why the doors were not opening. It just didn't make sense to me.

Although we were struggling financially, we were having such a good time enjoying a beautiful part of the country and feeling safe. Looking back, I have the fondest memories of living in the Hamptons. The people I met, the places I worked and lived, and the experiences Chelsea Laine and I shared were some of the best of my life! It was truly like living in a fairytale. I wouldn't have changed a thing.

DISCUSSION QUESTIONS:

1. What "small nudges" from God have helped guide you into a new chapter of life?

2. Can you recall a time when peace—not success—was the biggest sign that you were where God wanted you to be?

3. How has God used unexpected people or moments to bring healing to your heart?

Devotion Scripture: Isaiah 55:12 —*You will go out in joy and be led forth in peace.*

Reflection: Sometimes, the strongest sign that you're on the right path isn't certainty—it's peace. In the middle of fear, change, or uncertainty, God gently leads us forward with His quiet assurance.

Prayer: Lord, thank You for guiding me with Your peace, even when the road ahead is unclear. Help me to trust Your gentle nudges and follow wherever You lead. Amen.

CHAPTER EIGHTEEN

HELD THROUGH THE SHIFT

BACK TO TEXAS

Eventually, my money and, consequently, our fairy tale life came to an end. I felt desperate and had exhausted all my ideas to make money, so there seemed to be no other choice but to move back to Texas. Even though Chelsea Laine only had two or three weeks left of her eighth-grade year, we packed up and made the journey south. Chelsea Laine had made some really nice friends, and I had too, but I just didn't feel as if I had anywhere to turn. She had made such an impact on her friends and teachers that on her last day of school, the kids all got in a circle and hugged her and cried, even her teacher.

Looking back, I think this is one of the things I regret the most. What would have happened if I had just hung on a little longer, fought a little harder? I had just been hired at a really nice spa and was in training when the manager asked to see my license. I sheepishly had to tell him that I was actually only licensed in Texas and hadn't ever applied for reciprocity to gain my New York license. Why I didn't do that, I am not sure. Fear, probably. After living in fear and anguish for so long, even simple tasks—like filling out an application for reciprocity—sometimes felt like more than I could handle. Nobody had ever asked to see my license at the other salons I had worked in during my time in New York, so I decided it wasn't a big deal. I was just taking my chances, I guess. Regardless, my lack of New York licensing caused the door to slam shut on that employment opportunity.

Discouraged, I trekked back to Texas, even though I would have been starting a job teaching tennis in just a few short weeks. I guess the move back to Texas was motivated mostly by fear due to the fact that I did not take the time to pray and listen to God. I just did what I felt was best at the time. And, maybe it wouldn't have mattered at all—it could have just been God's plan all along for me to move back home. I will never know what could have happened if I had just been patient.

We can always learn from our past. I was confused and upset about moving back to Texas. All it reminded me of was fear, failure, chaos, and heartache. The only thing that was good about it was being near our family and friends again and going back to Fellowship Church in Dallas, which Chelsea Laine had been attending since she was in the fifth grade.

FINDING OUR FOOTING AGAIN

When we first moved back, I felt very out of place and lost. We stayed with one of my best friends, who was like an uncle to Chelsea Laine, Randy. We had met years before on a dating site and dated for a few months, but soon realized that we were better off as friends. We went dancing and had a lot of fun together. He went to church with us regularly, which was so nice. Randy was remodeling a large house in North Dallas and was nice enough to invite us to stay with him until we could figure out where we were going to live.

I had no choice but to go back to the job that I knew well in cosmetics at Nordstrom in the Galleria. I loved the store, but working retail was not what I desired. I was used to being a business owner and setting my own hours. But I was desperate and wanted to provide the best life I could for Chelsea Laine. A close friend of mine and former coworker, Robin, had told me about the Grand Spa in North Dallas. She knew the owner and offered to put in a good word for me. I was offered a position there as an esthetician and was allowed to offer permanent makeup services, as well. As the only artist at the salon, I was very busy with clients and grateful for this job. I was making around $3,500 a month, and sometimes more if I did someone's permanent makeup at my home instead of in the salon. At that time, this was enough for us to have a comfortable life, and I was able to provide for Chelsea Laine on my own.

Ever since Ben gave up his rights to Chelsea Laine, I had been the only provider for us. Now that I was making enough, we were able to get our own place. We moved back to North Dallas since my job was nearby. I thought Chelsea Laine would be going to a school in Richardson that specialized in an art and creative program, where her good friend and neighbor, Sarah, went to school. Unfortunately, it just wasn't the environment the girls needed at the time. Sarah lasted one day, and Chelsea Laine lasted two days at that school. Unfortunately, we were living too far north of Chelsea Laine's old school, so we decided to embark on a brand-new adventure of homeschooling. We chose to use a DVD-based accredited curriculum through *Abeka*, and Chelsea Laine absolutely loved it! The classes were recorded, but not live, and she thought it was funny to raise her hand and say, "I know the answer!" or, "I need to go to the bathroom," even though all she had to do was push "pause" on the DVD player. She thrived being homeschooled!

During the summer following our return to Texas, Chelsea Laine and I volunteered at Fellowship Church during their Vacation Bible School. We met a man in his late 30s named Blake, who attended our church and was volunteering that summer. He was blonde, of a smaller frame but very fit, and very likable. He and Chelsea Laine had very similar humor and would talk and respond back and forth like they were doing a *Saturday Night Live* skit.

One day, he told me about a product called Max GXL, a gluta-thione inhibitor. Blake and his friend Ty were business partners in this network marketing business, and it sounded very interesting to me. I love the community of network marketing, with people who encourage you to help you grow a business and make an income. I attended a presentation they had invited me to and decided to start promoting it, too. A few months into this journey, I had signed up 16 people! I received a call from the company asking if they could interview me about my achievements. I was so proud of myself and flattered that they would want to interview me! The article was published in the company newsletter. I felt celebrated, and really appreciated the extra income this network marketing company opportunity had given me and Chelsea Laine. God was so faithful to continue giving me these little nudges to try new things, and He would provide for me through them even when I didn't understand all of the steps.

Through Max GXL, we met Ty, another company self-starter. Ty lived in a really nice high-rise called the Ashton in one of my favorite areas of Dallas. One night, we were out to dinner at a restaurant in the Crescent Court, and Ty heard thirteen-year-old Chelsea Laine sing. He was so impressed that he put together a little band so she could sing. They called it *Chelsea Laine & Rachel*—named after her best friend—and they spent nearly the entire year rehearsing. They were very good, but only had the chance to rehearse in a real studio a few times. Chelsea Laine's cousin, Savannah, joined the band as well. Those girls were together all the time, either singing on the praise team for the youth group or practicing for their own band. I'm so thankful that Ty, our talented songwriter friend, spoke into the lives of these teenage girls and gave them such a fun and wholesome experience.

Sometimes, while we were living there, my oldest sister Ann stayed with us for a month or two. She had broken up with her boyfriend in New York and needed some time to decide on her next steps. For the most part, it was really nice having her there. She is a talented cook and made delicious meals for us, and helped out wherever and however she could. We were back in our home church, volunteering and attending every week. Our church put on a couple of events each year; FLAVOUR was an event for women, and C3 (Creative Pastors Conference), to which I had attended at least six or seven times. The C3 conference was so life-giving to me! Pastors from all over the world came to attend and speak at the two-day event. Though I didn't really understand it at the time, I just felt drawn to be there. Looking back now, I can see God's hand in it all.

Things were going pretty smoothly until the fall of 2008. I was enjoying working at Nordstrom, but in my heart, I felt like I wanted a change in my life and career. I felt like I was on autopilot; doing fine, but not really thriving. I was stuck in a rut and yearned for a way out.

That fall, the economy crashed, and my income was almost instantly cut in half. My rent alone consumed most of what I was now earning, so once again I found myself struggling to figure something else out for us to survive. I begged the manager of our apartment complex to let me move into a smaller, more affordable apartment, just so I could afford to pay the rent, but they would not let me out of my lease! They treated me like a common criminal or drug addict and offered no help whatsoever. It was like nobody had ever gone through tough financial times. I later filed a complaint with the company, and they officially apologized.

LIGHTS OUT, CANDLES ON

I received a call from our electric company one Thursday, reminding me that my bill was overdue. I was not in a position to pay the full bill, but after talking with them and explaining my situation, I worked out a plan to pay half of the bill that day and the balance on Monday after I got my next paycheck. They took half of the payment directly out of my checking account that afternoon… And the next day we awoke to no electricity. I was furious! *What happened to our agreement?!* I called them to ask what had happened, and they said something to the effect of, "I'm sorry, you will have to wait till Monday!" In all of the years of being a single mother, this had never happened. I felt so disappointed and embarrassed in myself, as if I were the worst mother on earth! It didn't feel fair.

One of my best friends from high school was Shelley. She had been in and out of touch with me over the years. That day, she happened to call, and I found myself telling her what had happened. She had struggled with addiction over the years, but she knew she could always count on me to be an open door, a listening ear, and a soft place to land when she needed it. She was finally clean and sober after 20 years of struggling with addiction, and we had rebuilt a sweet and meaningful friendship. At a time when I felt like my life was at the bottom of the barrel—sitting in the dark and convinced I was the worst mother on the planet—she said to me, "Erika! It's okay! Who cares? It's not like you need much light for tonight. Light some candles and have some fun!"

She continued, "The electricity going out doesn't make you a bad mom. It happened to us growing up, and my mom is amazing!" I nearly burst into tears, grateful for such a friend who would speak into my life in this way. Her words definitely lightened my heart and calmed my mind. She has always been there to lift me up and make me laugh in times of need, just at the right time.

This did make me feel better, but I was still determined to have electricity over the weekend. I'm pretty resourceful and have been blessed with having some of the best friends in many different professions, so I called one of my best guy friends, Jeremy (known to most of my friends as Foxy Arms). We had met in 1999, many years prior, at the Premier Club in Dallas, off Central Expressway, when I was working at the salon and he was working as a trainer in the gym. I saw him one day walking across the gym floor as he was playing basketball and told a coworker, "Oh my... Look at those foxy arms!" To my horror, she went and told him what I had said that night while we were all out after work. He turned to me and said, "So... Foxy arms, huh?" I must have turned three shades of red. We became fast friends, and I was so grateful for all the years he had helped Chelsea Laine and me, probably almost every time we moved, and even babysat a few times. He was like an uncle to Chelsea Laine, just a genuinely nice guy who was always there for us.

Jeremy remodeled houses. I called him and told him what was going on and that our electricity was out. I remembered him telling me that he had turned his on a while back. So he proceeded to tell me how to do it. Our apartment was in plain view of the leasing office, so I had to be discreet. As I held the phone up to my ear with my shoulder, I began to follow the steps he was telling me. Chelsea Laine was on the lookout to make sure none of the leasing agents were driving by on their golf carts. My adrenaline was on overdrive, and I had to duck behind the bushes a couple of times to escape being caught. I don't know if I was excited or terrified of what I was doing, but I knew that it wasn't fair what the electric company had done to me, so I wasn't going to stand for their mistakes and be without electricity for the whole weekend. Finally, I said, "Chelsea Laine, go inside and flip the light switch and see if it works." A few seconds later, she said, "It's on!" We cheered with joy!

Later that day, I noticed a police car parked at the leasing office. My stomach lurched as I thought, *Oh gosh… They found out!* I closed my blinds and hid inside my apartment until they were gone. It wasn't really why they were there, but looking back, I still laugh about it. When Monday came around, I paid the other half of my bill like I had said I would, and I never heard from the electric company again. I wonder if the electrician laughed to himself when he came out to turn my power back on and discovered that it had already been meddled with.

DISCUSSION QUESTIONS:

1. Have you ever made a big decision out of fear instead of faith? What was the result, and how did God use it in your life?

2. Looking back at your own regrets, how have you seen God's hand redeem situations you thought were failures?

3. In times of hardship, what role have friends, family, or your faith community played in helping you keep going?

Devotional Scripture: Isaiah 26:3-4 — *You will keep in perfect peace those whose minds are steadfast, because they trust in you. Trust in the Lord forever, for the Lord, the Lord himself, is the Rock eternal.*

Reflection: So often, like in this chapter, fear can drive our decisions when faith feels too hard. We think we have to figure everything out on our own, but God invites us to trust Him—even when the path feels unclear. Mistakes, regrets, and "what ifs" do not disqualify us from God's plan. He is able to take even our missteps and weave them into His greater purpose.

Prayer: Heavenly Father, thank You for being faithful even when I am fearful. Help me to bring my decisions before You instead of rushing ahead in my own strength. Teach me to trust that You are guiding my steps, even when I can't see the outcome. Thank You for providing for me in unexpected ways and surrounding me with people who encourage me. In Jesus' Name, Amen.

CHAPTER NINETEEN

LEARNING, HEALING, AND FORGIVENESS

AN INVITATION TO HEALING

One of my best childhood friends, Dantia, told me about a program called *The Road Adventure* while she was staying at my apartment during a time of marital strife. She could not go into the details, but I saw the deep and emotional changes it made in her. She offered to sponsor me if I would sign up for part one of the program, so I did. I remember thinking after the first session that weekend, *Gosh, I don't have any major problems like those people*. I haven't had an abortion. I had not been raped or molested. I have not been abandoned by my parents. I do not have an addiction... Or any of the other terrible stories that I heard that first evening. I wasn't even sure that I would continue with the rest of the sessions that weekend, but ultimately I decided to finish out my commitment. I am so thankful that I chose to stay the course! What a life-changing experience it turned out to be. I went through all three parts consecutively, which

I strongly recommend that anyone considering the program should do the same. Like my husband Erik explained, it's not so much what you get out of it but even more about what you are able to leave behind and are available to move forward with a healthy and happy life.

I can't share too many details about the program, because I wouldn't want to spoil the experience if you decide to attend. But what I can share with you are the ways it brought healing into my life. As I was going to one of the exercises, someone asked me if I had forgiven my ex-husband. I replied, "I've already forgiven his parents." Then someone else asked me the same question for the second time a few minutes later, and I answered the same way. When I said the words out loud, I realized that they were not asking me if I had forgiven my ex-in-laws. I soon realized that I, in fact, had not forgiven Ben.

We were working on one particular exercise, and my trainer said to me, "You have a wall built up so high nobody's getting through." I looked at him in complete shock. I truly felt like I was an open book. Ben had hurt me so deeply and for so many consecutive years and in so many different ways that I learned to just live with it and put my mind on autopilot. All the while, he did some of the most embarrassing and painful things, so it was normal to paint a picture of happiness to the outside world. As I chose to be happy and optimistic and buried all of the pain and hurt, I convinced myself that no one can really hurt me that badly—especially not someone who said they had once loved me, someone who was my first sexual experience, and especially someone that I chose to marry, right?

It's amazing how one word, one sentence, or what might seem like a small encounter can wreak havoc on your entire life, and you may not be aware of it. I learned about forgiveness on a level I had never before been taught. We learned that forgiveness was not for the other person, but for us to keep from being held prisoner by those hurts. *The Road Adventure* also taught me the tools to use so that I could "let go" for good.

THE BREAKING POINT OF FORGIVENESS

On my way home from the event that evening, not long after I got on the highway, I thought, maybe I should give what I learned today a try. The thought of actually doing this brought tears to my eyes. I began to speak aloud each of the things Ben had done to us, or situations he caused, that I knew must be forgiven. The truth was, I didn't really want to forgive him for anything. I was angry, and I truly wanted him to hurt as badly as he had hurt us. I began to literally yell out all of the horrible things that he had done to Chelsea Laine and me; it caused us so much pain and embarrassment. At the end of each sentence, I would say, "I forgive you." I probably should not have even been driving because the tears were so big in my eyes that I could barely see the lines on the road. This went on for at least five full minutes.

I hardly recognized my voice as I forced myself to scream out forgiveness that only myself and God would hear. Almost evil-sounding, my voice was gravelly and raspy, saturated with tears and sobs. Years of pent-up anguish and anger flowed out of me like a rushing river whose dam had broken. With each violent phrase of forgiveness, I felt my anger leave my body in short, sharp little bursts. Over a decade has passed since I forgave Ben once and for all, and I know now that this was deliverance in action.

Deliverance occurs when an unclean spirit (demon) releases its hold on an individual or ceases its harassment and leaves the person. When you have come into alignment with Jesus by submitting every part of your life to the blood and the authority of Christ, then Satan's legal right to have presence in your life is nullified. When this has been accomplished, believers may command these spirits to leave by the authority of Jesus Christ. As you command spirits to leave, you should have faith that they are doing so because you are commanding in the authority of the King of Kings and the Lord of Lords. They may exit with or without you experiencing any physical or sensory sensation. You will simply know they are gone when you realize that something is different in your life over the next few days or weeks. You may simply feel a sense that something has left you and that you feel lighter.

How many times do you have to forgive somebody who has hurt you? The Apostle Peter asked this question of Jesus in the Gospel of Matthew, Chapter 18.

Then Peter came to Jesus and asked, 'Lord, how many times shall I forgive my brother or sister who sins against me? Up to seven times?' Jesus answered, 'I tell you, not seven times, but seventy-seven times' (v. 21-22, NIV).

Of course, Jesus did not mean a literal seventy-seven times. Jesus was saying, essentially, "As many times as it takes." You have to forgive somebody as many times as it takes to no longer be emotionally tied to the act or feeling. You see, forgiving somebody does not mean that you have to establish a relationship with the person you are forgiving, nor does it mean that you approve of anything they did, but rather allows you to be set free and break the chains that have had you bound. It is healthy to have protective boundaries in place, but that doesn't mean that true, freeing forgiveness is not possible.

If you add up all of the things that I had gone through in our marriage and in the six years we dated prior, I believe that the most damaging words Ben ever spoke to me were, "I will kill you bitch." In my eyes, you are supposed to think of your husband as someone who is going to love you, protect you, care for you, and be gentle with you. I didn't realize it at the time, but when Ben said that to me, it killed my trust not just in him, but in every man. This had trapped me in distrust, anger, and unforgiveness until it had nearly smothered me and my entire life. When I finally decided to surrender and make a conscious choice to actively forgive Ben, I finally could move on with a healthy, happy life.

I challenge you to take some time today and think of who has hurt you. Do not waste another moment allowing that hurt to ruin your life and potentially block the blessings God has waiting for you!

This and other exercises in The Road Adventure study impacted my life in transformational ways. Another exercise was in learning about spiritual gifts and how God would use them through me.[6] My group leader mentioned to me that one of my spiritual gifts was my mouth, or my voice. I didn't really understand the concept at the time, but as I sought to understand, it slowly unfolded.

LETTING GO OF THE PAST

I also realized through *The Road Adventure* that I had subconsciously locked Chelsea Laine in my mind, emotionally, around eight years old. There were times that she would say to me, "Mom! I'm not five years old. I'm not little anymore." I truly felt like I was allowing her to be independent; however, she told me this several times. You see, when all of the trauma in her life started, she was around eight years old, and I suppose I went into survival mode.

Although this is a natural thing to do as a mother, it was time for me to change my thoughts and let this type of thinking go. After all, I had forgiven Ben, and now I needed to take care of the emotional part of letting go. When I went home that night, I sat down to talk with Chelsea Laine. I told her what I had discovered and asked her if she would forgive me. I told her that I didn't realize I was doing that. She just smiled at me and said, "Oh, Mom, I forgive you! You're fine." She said it with such calm and grace in her voice, like it was no worry at all. I was so grateful to learn and realize what I was doing and how to fix it. Growing, learning, and moving forward into God's plan and purpose is the best feeling. Letting go of the trauma that has happened to you is life-changing. I encourage you to check out *The Road Adventure* for yourself. If you are brave enough to sign up, you won't regret it! Don't wait!

For more information about *The Road Adventure* events and other resources, check out https://www.theroadadventure.org/

DISCUSSION QUESTIONS:

1. Who in your life have you struggled to forgive, and what's been the hardest part of letting go?

2. How does understanding that forgiveness is for your freedom—not the other person's—change your perspective?

3. What spiritual or emotional "walls" might God be inviting you to bring down so He can heal you?

Devotional Scripture: Ephesians 4:32 — *Be kind and compassionate to one another, forgiving each other, just as in Christ God forgave you.*

Reflection: Forgiveness doesn't mean forgetting what happened or trusting someone who hasn't changed. It means releasing the hold that pain has on your heart. When we forgive, we aren't saying what happened was okay—we are saying that it will no longer have the power to define our future.

Prayer: Lord Jesus, I give You the hurt that has weighed me down for too long. Help me to release it into Your hands. Teach me to forgive freely, just as You have forgiven me. Break every chain of bitterness or resentment that keeps me from living in the fullness of Your joy. Amen.

CHAPTER TWENTY

A BOND SHAPED BY LOSS

FROM FRIENDSHIP TO SOMETHING MORE

Back in my younger years, Paige, one of my dearest friends from high school passed away suddenly, along with her unborn child. It was devastating news—so unexpected, so heartbreaking. I remember the phone call, the disbelief, and the tears that came before I could even process what I'd heard. We had been planning to celebrate a joyful milestone in her life, but instead, we gathered to grieve.

Her loss left a mark on everyone who knew her. She had a light about her—one of those rare souls who could make anyone feel welcome and seen. I have often thought back on our friendship and the moments we shared, wishing I had one more chance to tell her how much she meant to me.

That tragedy created a bond among our friend group, especially with one friend in particular, Jay. We had known each other since high school, and though life had taken us in different directions, shared grief has a way of reconnecting people. Over time, our friendship deepened, and years later, it would lead to an unexpected chapter in my life.

FROM FRIENDSHIP TO SOMETHING MORE

In the summer of 2009, I started talking to an old friend from high school named Jason. "Jay" and I had been a part of the same friend group and had many fond memories over the years. He had been engaged following high school to my friend Paige, who I mentioned earlier had been tragically killed in a freak accident. I think that accident created a sort of bond between all of us as friends, as tragedy often does.

Jay and I had stayed in touch off and on throughout the years, but we began talking regularly over the phone when he was living in Sturgis, South Dakota. It was fun catching up with him, and it wasn't long before he asked me if I wanted to come up and visit during the Sturgis Rally. I knew the rally was a motorcycle thing, but not much more than that. I said, "I can't go anywhere for that long unless I'm working." He offered me a job bartending at his restaurant for a couple of weeks, and I accepted. Although it seemed odd to be away from Chelsea Laine for that long, she was in the 9th grade and would be happy to stay with family and close friends. I knew she would be just fine, so I packed my bags and headed north. It was a fun two weeks, and Jay and I grew closer. I had always loved him as a friend, and now we were moving that friendship into a relationship. I can't say that I was in love *with* him, but I had a deep love for him due to our longstanding history together.

A FRESH START IN THE BLACK HILLS

A couple of weeks after I got back home, on a phone conversation, Jay asked if I would like to move to South Dakota permanently. It didn't take me long to make my decision. I was ready for a change! It didn't work out in the Hamptons, so maybe this would be the much-needed move Chelsea Laine and I needed. Since she was homeschooled, she wasn't really involved in other activities. My job at the time was not really anything with a future. I was just ready for a change! The only thing that we were sad to leave was our church family, friends, and our family, of course, and Chelsea Laine's youth pastor, Kevin, and the youth group. But the need to get away and start over was just too strong. It was necessary for us.

Even during that season of change, we stayed deeply rooted in our church. Chelsea Laine was thriving in her youth group, *The Mix*—singing on the praise and worship team, volunteering, and building friendships that lit up her life. Her youth pastor, Kevin, was a constant source of love, guidance, and encouragement. I still say he's one of my favorite people. Knowing she had that kind of spiritual mentor and community meant the world to me.

On the first visit with Jay in South Dakota, I fell in love with the Black Hills. The cool weather and the mountains were breathtaking! Though I had forgiven Ben, Texas still reminded me of all of the sadness and trauma we had been through, and I just wanted a fresh start. Jay's invitation to move to South Dakota seemed to be just the open door we needed.

FAITH, FRIENDSHIP, AND PLANTING SEEDS

At this time, Chelsea Laine and her dad did not have any kind of relationship at all. Ben had called her a few times, but their conversations were always very strange, and Chelsea Laine seemed to accept the fact that she was estranged from him. Though it saddened me that this was a reality of her life, I had so much peace knowing she didn't have to deal with any of his drama or bipolar behaviors.

Once again, we said goodbye to our family, friends, and church family. We stuffed my Jeep full of our most-needed items, put our furniture and other items into long-term storage, and hit the road. The apartment we lived in at the time would not let me break my lease, even though so many people had suffered financially from the 2008-2009 economic crash. They told me that they would rent it out as soon as possible, and if that happened, I wouldn't be responsible for the remainder of my lease. That never did happen, so I still had to pay thousands of dollars even after I moved out. It was frustrating, but I was not going to let this setback keep us from moving.

Chelsea Laine and I set out for our new adventure! It was late August, and with our little Parti-Pomeranian, Bella Bear, by our side, we were on our way to South Dakota. It was a 16-hour drive. We stopped halfway and spent the night in Nebraska at a really nice bed and breakfast. With a lot of our things on top of our Jeep, we thought it would be safer there than in a hotel. It was a gorgeous Victorian Home with a giant wrap-around porch, and our room was on the upper level. We got settled in to sleep, but in the middle of the night, Bella started growling, then barking. This was out of character for her and really scared us! I jumped up and turned on the light. I'm not sure what was in that room, evil spirits? Who knows, but I prayed and tried to go back to sleep, but couldn't. I even kept the light on!

The next day, as we were driving, Chelsea Laine and I kept seeing billboards for Murdo, SD. It had a huge old-time car on it. We must have seen the signs for this place for a couple of hours, and then all of a sudden, there it was! We had arrived in Murdo, South Dakota. We decided to exit and see what this long, old car thing was all about. We had to pull over on the side of the road because we were laughing so hard. Seriously, it was the funniest thing to us, and to this day, we always have a laugh over "The Old-Time Car."

Driving into South Dakota was so beautiful. We passed the Badlands, which are a barren region covering an area of 2,000 square miles, and are colorful rock formations from millions of years ago. The terrain was so different from the areas of Texas where I grew up. As we got closer to the Black Hills, to me it looked like the land of milk and honey—a promised land of beauty. There were miles and miles of rolling hills dotted with groupings of large, beautiful trees. In the distance, we could see the isolated mountain range rising from the Great Plains of North America in western South Dakota, extending into Wyoming.

We drove through Rapid City, where the main airport is, the same airport I had flown in just a few weeks earlier. Chelsea Laine had a bit of culture shock, unsure of her new home and what she had agreed to by moving to this small-town area of the world. Chelsea Laine had grown up in downtown Dallas and spent middle school in Highland Park, so moving to a small town was a whole new experience for her. I'll never forget the moment we drove down Sturgis's main street, and she spotted a shiny sports car. She grinned and said, "Okay, I guess this place is alright." I couldn't help but laugh—it was such a classic Chelsea Laine way of finding the silver lining.

Our first stop was Roscoz Steak House, the restaurant that Jay and his parents owned. Chelsea Laine met Jay for the first time, finally getting to put a face to the name in all the stories and memories I had shared with her. We went to Jay's house and got settled in our rooms. Jay knew of the situation between Ben and me, and Chelsea Laine and I felt very protected by staying with him. Jay helped us get on our feet in more ways than one. He gave us the new start that we needed.

NEW ROUTINES AND SMALL-TOWN LIFE

Life was good. With Jay's encouragement, I registered Chelsea Laine in Sturgis High School, which turned out to be a wonderful decision. Autumn came, and Chelsea Laine was settling into school and meeting new friends, while I worked at the restaurant with Jay and was happy to be doing something completely different. I did a little bit of everything at the restaurant. My favorite job was helping out the waitresses by going around to each table and visiting with customers, making sure they had everything they needed. The previous year, I had volunteered for a summer retreat at Allaso Ranch (part of Fellowship Church) and had worked in the kitchen, so it was fun to see how God had been preparing me for what was to come. Jay's parents, Billy and Nancy, were also at the restaurant quite a bit, mainly helping on weekends. Whenever they came, Nancy brought out her magnificent, homemade, delicious desserts, and Billy made his famous chili. We had a lot of fun working together and would visit for an hour after closing over a glass of wine.

Then the snow came, and it was winter. South Dakota had an unusually large amount of snow that year. I remember that it was up to my waist in the front yard! When it snows in South Dakota, thankfully, they have all of the heavy equipment to clear the roads so you can go about your business as usual. This was in stark contrast to Texas, where no equipment and black ice is a recipe for the world shutting down! Needless to say, it was an adjustment moving to a far northern climate when I had primarily only known Texas weather for the majority of my life.

Sturgis was a town of only 6,000 in population, give or take a few. At the time, I didn't know much about the area other than when I came up for the Sturgis Motorcycle Rally. The only other part of

South Dakota I knew, other than Sturgis, was a brief trip we had taken through Spearfish Canyon and the Latchstring Restaurant to have lunch and look out at the beautiful scenery following my two-week work adventure at the rally. The canyon is beautiful and soon became my favorite place in the northern Black Hills.

Chelsea Laine easily made new friends at Sturgis High School. Previously accustomed to a large school of over 2,000 students, she quickly became popular in a class of 200 with her friendly personality and contagious smile. She soon became known as "Chelsea Laine Barbie" and personalized her car's license plate to read: "SDBAR-BIE." The fashion difference from Dallas to small-town Sturgis was night and day, and I'm not sure the other students had seen anybody come to school before dressed like they were stepping out of a magazine.

I believe her first best friends were Danielle and Stephanie, two very sweet girls who came from really nice families. One day, she and Danielle pulled up in front of our house, and I came out to talk with them. As I got closer, I saw the window open a little, and Chelsea Laine tried to throw out a cigarette to hide it from me. Unfortunately for her, I saw it as it rolled down the glass window and sat on the ledge of the car, still lit. I was appalled, and they were in shock! I was so upset as I didn't know or had ever seen her smoking before. It was probably something she was just trying out, but I wasn't having it, and that was the end of it. To this day, fourteen years later, we still laugh about this mishap.

I will say that raising her in a high school in a new town where I didn't know any of the other parents personally was really challenging! It was tough to gauge what kind of background they had. Was she safe with them? It is in these situations in life that you have to call on God for comfort and step out in faith and live in a place of peace instead of fear! At the end of her sophomore year, she told me that she was going to try out to be a cheerleader. I was sort of nervous because in Texas, you have to be able to be experienced—nearly Olympic level—in gymnastics. That might be a slight exaggeration, but in Texas, they take cheerleading and tumbling *very* seriously. Nevertheless, she was excited to try out, so when she had made up her mind, I just cheered her on (pun intended).

The day of the tryouts came, and when I didn't hear from her, I called the school to ask one of the Pams (for there were two of them) in the front office if she had made it. She wouldn't tell me. She just said, "They just announced it." Chelsea Laine came into the office, got on the phone, and said, "Mom, I made it!" Although I was so relieved and happy for her later that afternoon, the thought of the expenses for her uniforms crossed my mind. In Texas, I knew friends who had to come up with over a thousand dollars for uniforms and such, but soon found out that in South Dakota, all uniforms (except for undergarments and shoes) were paid for by the school district. *Whew!* Chelsea Laine really enjoyed her experience at Sturgis High School, cheering at football and wrestling games, and participating in competition-level cheer during her junior and senior years.

No matter how dismal a situation seemed, God always found a way to bless us all along our journey. I feel that it is so imperative to look for and focus on the good things in life and continuously choose to have a grateful heart to be able to recognize all of these situations as blessings.

FAITH, FRIENDSHIP, AND PLANTING SEEDS

Even though I enjoyed working at Roscoz, I began thinking about going back to work at a salon. There was a non-denominational church called Countryside that I had started attending. While it wasn't quite what we were used to, we were glad to be back attending regular services and enjoying corporate worship with like-minded friends.

I found opportunities to read the Bible to Jay from time to time and even got him to come to a Christmas service. I really felt that God moved us to South Dakota and had us there for many reasons. Where Jay was concerned, I felt a deep longing to show him the love in my heart for God. Hopefully, it would lead him to an understanding that God didn't cause his late fiancé's death, and to possibly find a way for him to let some of his anger and sadness go from the loss of his late fiancé and their unborn baby. I prayed that Jay may be able to trust in God again so that he could heal, be happy, and be the Jay I once knew in high school. I think Jay has been happier since then, and I'm glad I could have planted a seed of hope.

We are all called to share God's love and grace with anyone He puts in our path. Don't ever let an opportunity pass you by when you feel that nudge from God to pray for someone or to share a testimony of how He helped you in your life.

Always be prepared to give an answer to everyone who asks you to give the reason for the hope that you have (1 Peter 3:15, NIV).

As time went on, I realized that Jay and I were more friends than lovers, and Chelsea Laine and I found a place of our own. Moving out of Jay's house and finding our own place was really good for us. While I was so grateful for the safe landing space staying with Jay had been, we all agreed it was in our friendship's best interest to be just that, friends. What mattered most to us was preserving a life-long friendship rather than forcing a romantic relationship that wasn't truly there. He is a mountain man, and I am a little fancy!

DISCUSSION QUESTIONS:

1. How did Erika and Chelsea Laine's move to South Dakota reflect both faith and fresh beginnings?

2. In what ways did Erika recognize God's hand in the transition, even through difficulty?

3. Have you ever had to leave behind something comfortable to follow a new path God was placing before you?

Devotional Scripture: Isaiah 43:2 — *When you pass through the waters, I will be with you; and when you pass through the rivers, they will not sweep over you.*

Reflection: Even when the journey is unfamiliar, God is already there preparing the way. Sometimes, He uses changes in location, relationships, and seasons to do the deeper work of healing and hope.

Prayer: Lord, thank You for going before me in every transition. Help me trust You in new seasons, and give me eyes to see Your hand in the unfamiliar.

CHAPTER TWENTY-ONE

HEALING AND RESTORATION

FINDING OUR HOME

One day, as I was on a flight home from Dallas after I had been back visiting, I was seated next to a woman who quickly became my first closest girlfriend there in South Dakota. As Danielle and I talked, we realized our birthdays were on the same day, May 11, and that we attended the same church. I don't think we ever stopped talking on that two-hour flight. We were like little girls, giggling, laughing, and sharing stories. I told her that I had been in the beauty industry for many years and was looking for a place to work. She told me about a salon that she knew of in Spearfish called Sonya's Salon that may be hiring.

When I got back to Spearfish, I went to Sonya's for an interview. They didn't need an esthetician, but they did need a nail artist. Though I could do nails in my sleep, it had been years since I had done them professionally. Sonya's was a small and quaint salon, and

I decided it would be a good next step as I moved on from my relationship with Jay. I accepted the position and felt extremely happy about my decision. I was also able to offer permanent makeup on the days Sonya's sister was not using her space.

There was just one problem: I didn't have my South Dakota license (Remember how that played out in New York?). I was going to have to go back to school and take the South Dakota test. I called "the powers that be" a few times, begging them to see if there was another way to go about it so I didn't have to go back to school at ground zero after over 20 years in the profession. One day, my persistence paid off, and the lady at the South Dakota Board of Licensing said, "How much continuing education do you have?"

I replied, "A lot!"

After explaining a bit more, she said, "I think we will be able to use those hours, so you will just have to take a written test!" I was ecstatic, and this enabled me to get to work right away.

That Sunday after church, Chelsea Laine and I drove around Spearfish looking for a place to live. We found a quadruplex house that was brand new. It wasn't even fully finished yet, but I was determined to live there, as it was in a really nice neighborhood. I walked into the building and talked to a man who was working on the finish-out. He told me that the owner did not live in Spearfish but gave me his phone number. I called and asked if I could rent his place. I was ready to move, so I was pretty direct in asking. He told me that he didn't even know what he would charge, so I took it upon myself to tell him what I could afford. Believe me, when I tell you that this was a God-thing, it was. I explained my situation, that I was from Texas and was starting all over, and that if he would agree on $625 for the next six months to a year, he could raise the rent after that. Remarkably, he agreed and never raised the rent. I'm sure he could have gotten at least $800-$900 for our two-bedroom, one bathroom apartment.

Chelsea Laine and I had been through so many transitions by this point that anything put in front of us was simply like a new adventure. At least, that's the way we chose to look at it. As we got settled in, we laughed a lot and quoted movies like usual for entertainment. I think all of these "new adventures" helped to curate the special bond Chelsea Laine and I have to this day.

PROVISION WITH PURPOSE

The only issue with moving to Spearfish was that Chelsea Laine still went to school in Sturgis, which was about 15 miles away. I felt bad about her having to drive that far, but I knew that I didn't want to live in Sturgis. Spearfish was much closer to the style of living that I was used to, with cute little coffee shops and boutiques.

My friend Danielle and I started working out together at Barefoot Fitness, and soon after, I did her permanent eyeliner. One by one, the people in our fitness class started flowing into the salon for me to do their permanent eyebrows, eyeliner, or lip blushing. It was amazing! I quickly built a good reputation and clientele. Working at Sonya's salon was where I met some of my best and closest friends, and to this day, we are still close girlfriends; I lovingly call them my South Dakota sisters. While I was doing pretty well financially, my credit score was still a dumpster fire after all that Ben had done. With Chelsea Laine's longer commute to school, I decided to purchase a vehicle for her. My friend Danielle mentioned that her husband owned a car dealership and she would put our needs on his radar. Her husband called and told me that the perfect car had come in for Chelsea Laine, a one-owner, newer model silver Honda Civic with low miles in a price range I could afford. I don't know if Robert pulled some strings for me or not, but I was able to secure a loan and purchase the car for Chelsea Laine. We bought the car one day before she was to return to school. Talk about being saved by grace!

COFFEE, COMMUNITY, AND CONTENTMENT

I loved my job at Sonya's and all the friends I met along the way. I had a short ten-minute commute to work in the beautiful scenery of Spearfish. Sometimes I would leave early and stop at one of my favorite little coffee shops, where I could just enjoy my peaceful life while drinking a coffee latte of the day. I felt as if I was living in another world, like in a storybook. I had finally found peace again with Chelsea Laine. We had our own place, attended church regularly, and invited friends to join us, so that they would know and feel God's love for them. My clientele continued to grow, and I felt so proud to be able to provide for the two of us. Truly, it was a miraculous blessing straight from God. He had once again made a way.

The steady business I had at the salon built my confidence back up, which was important since I had felt like such a failure from having been dragged through the dirt financially and emotionally for years. I remember going to see Chelsea Laine cheer at a football game in Sturgis. As I walked onto the bleachers, I swear, even though we were new to the area, I got waved to at least five or six times. Every one of them was a client for whom I had done permanent makeup. This made me feel as if I had found my home, a place I could build real, lasting relationships and finally prosper and grow.

I truly had found happiness and contentment living in the Black Hills of South Dakota.

MATCH.COM & MAD HATTERS

Though most of my friends were married, I did have a couple of single girlfriends, and we had fun going out together on weekends when Chelsea Laine was busy with her friends. I remember one year for Halloween, my friend Shannon, Sam, and Sonya's sister, and I hopped from Spearfish to Sturgis to Deadwood, entering three costume contests.

On some weekends, Chelsea Laine would go camping with friends. I thought this was really cool because back in Texas, we wouldn't think of camping—not ever! The heat and the bugs are a big NO for me. But, something about being in the Black Hills was such a different experience than living in the city, or even in the suburbs of Dallas, and it made us do things we hadn't ever done before.

She would also go up to a place called Gilded Mountain in Lead/Deadwood to a cozy cabin that her boyfriend's dad owned. We would often laugh about how, in Dallas, you had to worry about all the vehicle traffic, but in South Dakota, you worried about wildlife jumping onto the road or your car slipping on the snow and ice. What a different world!

DISCUSSION QUESTIONS:

1. What small blessings began to show up in Erika's life during this time?

2. How can routine and structure be a form of healing?

3. What does restoration mean to you?

Devotional Scripture: Joel 2:25 — *I will repay you for the years the locusts have eaten.*

Reflection: Restoration doesn't always come with fanfare. Often, it arrives in the form of normalcy, steadiness, and peace.

Prayer: Lord, thank You for repaying what was lost. I receive Your restoration, even in the quiet seasons. Amen.

CHAPTER TWENTY-TWO

A LOVE RESTORED

A FACEBOOK FRIEND REQUEST THAT CHANGED EVERYTHING

One day, I noticed a friend request on Facebook from an old friend that I had known since we first met at Hastings Elementary. His name was Erik Williamson, and I hadn't seen or heard from him since I was over 20 years old, waiting for my oil to get changed at the shop near my house. (Remember that story?) Oh, the power of social media! I accepted the friend invite, and we chatted back and forth a little. We exchanged phone numbers, and one day he called me. I was in Rapid City, about 45 minutes from Spearfish, where I lived, and had just finished with my errands in town. It was so good to hear from him! If you recall, he had been my fifth-grade "boy-friend" and we were friends throughout elementary, junior high, and high school. The rest of our story unfolded like a *Hallmark* movie.

By the next day, Erik and I were inseparable. We would talk on the phone or text unless we were working or sleeping. I remember Chelsea Laine knocking on my door, saying, "Mom, are you in there?" She opened the door, smiled, and said, "Gosh! Who are you talking to?" Erik and I talked about old times, friends, and our lives. I talked about my relationship with God and all He had done in my life. I told Erik how Chelsea Laine and I had served in our home church and all of the miracles that had happened through growing my relationship with Jesus. He seemed to really respond to these stories. He believed in God, but didn't have the same depth of relationship with Him as I had come to have. Was I perfect? No, I was far from it, but I lived my life by putting God first and tried to be all that I could be for Him. I fell short, for sure, as we do as humans, but I was fully aware of my relationship with God, asking for His guidance, and regularly repented and asked for His forgiveness when needed. I knew that I couldn't have gotten through any of what I had been through if it were not for my close relationship with Jesus, attending church, and seeking spiritual mentors along the way.

FAITH CONVERSATIONS THAT DREW US CLOSER

I specifically remember Erik telling me about a time in his life when he was pretty confused and angry at God about some things that had happened to him. I asked him if he had talked to God about it. He seemed surprised and said, "Not really."

I said, "Well, did you know that you can yell at God?" He was taken aback by this notion, then I said, "He can handle it; He just wants you to come to Him. Tell Jesus your problems, surrender to Him, and He'll handle the rest!"

Erik still talks about the moment when I shared this with him and shares the same with others when the opportunity arises. I believe it changed his faith to understand that God just wants a daily relationship with you—nothing fancy, no rules, no rights or wrongs—just be honest in your desire to know Him. God will provide the way. If you step close to Him, He will step close to you.

A helpful scripture to give you hope is Psalm 32:8, which says, *I will instruct you and teach you the way you should go; I will counsel you with my eye upon you.*

AN UNEXPECTED ENGAGEMENT AND A WEDDING TO REMEMBER

We hadn't even been talking for three days before he made a proposition. "Hey, when you come back to Texas, maybe we can go to this beautiful area in Texas." He explained that it was an area where we could rent a cabin, and there were many fun activities to do.

I said, "Well, I'm probably going to regret this later, but for now I'm going to say no!"

On the fourth day of our rekindled relationship, Erik sent me a text that ended with, "Love ya!"

It made me smile, and I said, "Did you read what you just wrote?"

He said, "Yes, I said I love you!"

I was so happy and felt like my heart was complete because I knew I already loved him. Even though we hadn't been reconnected for long, I knew that he was "the one." I can't explain it other than... *I just knew.* Some people call it listening to your heart, others may call it your gut, but I have learned that these are God-moments. Peace and calm came over me, and everything just felt right.

It is still crazy to me as I think back to that little fifth-grade boy breaking up with me at the pencil sharpener, that here I was decades later, falling in love with him after a week of reconnecting. We had known each other basically our entire lives—double-dated on a limo ride during our senior prom, married (and divorced) other people—but yet, God was still working out His plan.

Isn't it crazy to look back at your life and see how so many things could have been different? For about the first few years of our marriage, I would frequently say, "Why didn't you call me back?" Or sometimes I would just simply apologize for turning him down.

The day after Erik told me he loved me, I decided to ask him my "safe question" in a text. It read, "Would you ever consider being married again?"

He answered back with a question, "Would you want to be my princess someday?"

I said, "I'd love to," and that was it! About five minutes later, I texted him a picture of the wedding ring that had been on my vision board for a few years, a princess cut pink stone set with diamonds around it from *Tiffany*! Later, I asked him if that scared him, and he said, "Not at all." Most guys would run for the hills if a girl texted them a ring!

We kept texting and talking about our possible future plans. I told him that I wanted to get married at the beach, and he agreed.

Just like that, after a week of phone calls and texting, we were engaged, even though we hadn't even seen each other in over 22 years. As I write this, it does seem unreal that everything happened the way that it did and so quickly, but it didn't at the time. I knew—*I knew*—that God had brought him into mine and Chelsea Laine's life. I felt a nudge from God again, so I stepped out in faith to follow.

At this point, Erik had never even met Chelsea Laine, but he assured me that he would love her as if she were his own daughter. He also said it would be an honor to one day give her the wedding of her dreams. *Who is this guy?* I thought, as Leanne Morgan would say, "What in the World?" Seriously, Chelsea Laine has to be the sweetest, kindest, beautiful, and most thoughtful, loving daughter on earth, and nobody in all of those years had ever said that to me.

I had told him that I was looking for my "Noah," like in the movie *The Notebook*, which is one of my favorite movies of all time!

Back then, people were still watching movies on DVD, so I thought it was appropriate to mail him one so that we could watch it "together." This was our first long-distance "date." Erik was my Noah.

A few days later, he booked a trip to South Dakota. It would be the first time we would lay eyes on each other in 22 years! I just couldn't believe I was engaged to such a sweet man. How had I known him my entire life but hadn't really seen him before now? The man I had always dreamed of, hoped for, and prayed for, yet he was even better than I could have ever imagined! God has a way of blessing people who are chasing after *His* heart. It might not come in the time frame you want, but in God's timing, it will be just right. Trust me, I know this firsthand.

On my birthday, May 11, 2011, I was working at Sonya's Salon. I heard someone come in through the door, and when I looked up, there was the most beautiful flower arrangement I had ever seen being delivered to me! I felt like I was living in a fairy tale. As I write this part of the story, it is now 13 years later, and I still feel that way, maybe even more so.

It was approximately two weeks later that I was to see my prince for the first time. I drove to the Rapid City Airport to pick up Erik. I was so nervous and excited. Thoughts and emotions swirled through my head. *What if he doesn't meet my expectations?* I mean, 22 years is a long time, and I had only seen two photos of him! Rapid City Airport is small, and was even smaller back then—so small that you can still wait for your loved ones to walk down that hallway and run and hug them! I was waiting with excitement, my phone to my ear with Erik on the line. I said, "Do you have on a black shirt?" He said he did, and I was thinking, "*Yes!*" He was perfectly handsome.

I couldn't believe this was happening to me. My eyes didn't move away from Erik as he walked closer and closer down the hallway towards me. When he finally came through the doors, I was bursting with joy! He was feeling the same. We embraced each other with a hug and then looked into each other's eyes, and then... Our first kiss in over 30 years! We were trembling with excitement. It was like we were in a dream. I just couldn't believe how happy I was at that moment.

We held hands as we walked to the car and for the entire ride back to Spearfish. It was as if the puzzle pieces we had been missing from our lives for the past couple of decades were finally found and put back together.

CHELSEA LAINE MEETS ERIK

We explored the area together and went to Spearfish Canyon Lodge for a couple of days. To this day, it is one of our most favorite places to visit or go for a staycation! It is a beautiful lodge with great service. The manager, Susan, has been there since we first started staying, and she has always been ready to accommodate us and any friends we've brought along over the years. There are hiking trails, waterfalls, UTVs to ride in the summer, and snowmobiles for the winter, which we have done a few times on Valentine's weekend. It's also where they shot the last scene of *Dances with Wolves*, which is one of our favorite movies. I believe Erik stayed in South Dakota for probably ten days on that first trip before going back to Dallas.

This was an exciting time because we were planning our destination wedding. We had decided on Cozumel, Mexico, for the location, as we had both been there before and knew how beautiful it was. Chelsea Laine was going to be a senior in the fall, so we decided to get married on August 5, 2011.

It was so much fun trying on wedding dresses; I just felt like a princess. Planning our destination wedding was so exciting, and when we got there, it was like I was on a reality TV show. The place we got married at planned everything, and it was so much fun and stress-free. We had our own suite and pool, which was so cool. We decided to have our wedding at sunset. Erik and I had written our own vows. He told me that he would love me like I had never known, and to this day, he has kept his word, and I get to live the dream I always prayed about. When I was reciting my vows, the emotions became real, and all of a sudden, I covered my face and was overwhelmed with happy tears. I just couldn't believe that this was happening. It was everything I had ever dreamed of.

It was a small wedding with our children standing by our sides and my parents walking me down the aisle, and many friends and family who came to support us. We had about 19 people, including ourselves, join us for our wedding. The whole day seemed surreal, and I was overwhelmed that this was my new reality. Our marriage was a long-distance marriage until the following spring of 2012 because it was Chelsea Laine's senior year, and I wanted her to finish out the year in Sturgis. It was actually pretty exciting. Although I missed Erik terribly, it turned out to be a fun adventure because he would come up to South Dakota about every ten days and stay for about the same amount of time. It kind of felt like we got an extended honeymoon. If I'm being honest, our entire marriage has felt like a honeymoon! I'm grateful for that.

It was so exciting counting down the days that he would be back in my arms and the opportunity to show him around the beautiful Black Hills each time he visited. We went to the Badlands, Mount Rushmore, Spearfish Canyon, Needles Highway, Sylvan Lake, Custer State Park, Devils Tower in Wyoming, and so many of our favorite places in Deadwood, Sturgis, and of course, my beloved Spearfish. I was able to introduce him to most of my close friends. For an anniversary present, I surprised him with an 1880 train ride from Hill City to Keystone all through the hills, followed by a helicopter ride over Mount Rushmore. On his trips back, we also enjoyed our favorite restaurants, skiing at Terry Peak, and attending "Friday Nights," a festival where they block off the downtown main street with a live band and venues in downtown Spearfish.

One of the highlights of Erik's life was that he was able to be in Sturgis for Chelsea Laine's senior walk. Since Ben had abandoned her, you can imagine how much I appreciated having a loving husband who was willing to step in and be the best and most supportive step-dad, more like a real father she had never known.

Our first Christmas as a married couple, Chelsea Laine and I traveled to Dallas to be with Erik's boys and my family. It was a nice homecoming to be with my husband around all of them for the first time. It had been just Chelsea Laine and me for so long that it was just a fun and exciting time.

LIFE BETWEEN TWO STATES

In the spring of 2012, following Chelsea Laine's graduation from high school, we made the tough decision to move back to Texas. Though I had a special love for South Dakota and all of its scenery, seasons, people, and simple way of life, it ultimately made more practical sense for us to live in Texas, where Erik's roofing and construction business was located. Following the move, I was able to retain clientele in South Dakota that would bring me back quarterly to the Black Hills.

For the last 12 years, I have traveled to and from Texas to South Dakota, taking care of my clients, working anywhere from three to five days, and then Erik flies up for a mini-vacation. My friends were surprised that I have continued to come back so often, but I truly wouldn't have it any other way! The beautiful thing about traveling back and forth for so many years is that I've been able to watch my dearest friends' babies be born and grow up. I've been able to attend their children's musical performances, basketball games, birthday parties, and now their graduations, and continue to be a part of their lives. They are truly my extended family, and this has brought me great joy!

Our first year in Texas, we found a home to rent that had a swimming pool (which is almost an essential for Texas living). Our property backed up to a beautiful Friesian horse ranch. It was different living out in the suburbs versus downtown Dallas, where I had raised Chelsea Laine. Although I was excited to be with my husband daily rather than continuing a long-distance relationship, I was struggling with finding my way living in the South again. Although Texas was my home, there were so many reminders of sadness, fear, struggle, and failure that crept back into my thoughts. Even though they had happened long ago, flashbacks would torment me, and I definitely felt like a fish out of water.

We were living about 20 minutes south of Dallas, and I wasn't sure if I wanted to return to the world I had left behind—working with plastic surgeons and dermatologists as a medical aesthetician—or if I should look for a position at a spa instead. Yet I didn't feel peace about either option. Most of my career had been spent freelancing, which came naturally to me since my parents had both owned their own businesses, and deep down I sensed that was still where I thrived best.

DISCUSSION QUESTIONS:

1. How did Erika's past prepare her for the love and companionship she found with Erik?

2. What role did faith and transparency play in their reconnection?

3. Have you ever experienced a divine delay that turned into a blessing?

Devotional Scripture: Psalm 37:4 — *Take delight in the Lord, and He will give you the desires of your heart.*

Reflection: God's timing isn't slow—it's precise. He doesn't just meet our needs; He restores our dreams when we least expect it.

Prayer: Lord, thank You for the unexpected blessings You bring in the right season. Help me to trust that what You have for me is better than anything I could plan on my own.

CHAPTER TWENTY-THREE

STRENGTHENING THE FOUNDATION

RETURNING TO THE HAMPTONS

Somewhere during this time, we rented a house in May in the Hamptons in New York for three weeks—probably 2013. This was right before Memorial Day, so the rates weren't sky-high yet. The high season for the Hamptons is Memorial Day to Labor Day, and I really wanted to go back to show Erik where I had lived. I'd also been feeling that nudge to write my book and tell my story, and I thought, *What better place to begin than in a quiet, peaceful setting like this?*

At the beginning of the trip, my childhood friend Lesly came with me and stayed for almost a week. Then Erik flew in. A few days later, one of my and Erik's best childhood friends, Ginger, and her husband, Phillip, along with her sister, Jackie, and her husband, joined us. They stayed for about a week of our three-week rental.

The rest of the time gave me the opportunity to be in a serene and beautiful place to think and begin writing. After all, this was a story I had felt I needed to share, but it wasn't one I really wanted to visit again—so it was challenging to say the least.

While we were there, I reached out to some of my friends from when I had lived there five years earlier. Life looked very different. Back then, Chelsea Laine and I had been scraping by financially, but this time, I was married, and we were eating at lavish restaurants, enjoying all the plush and beautiful surroundings of Sag Harbor, East Hampton, Bridgehampton, and Southampton.

We drove through Amagansett and ate at the famous Lobster Roll—yum, yum, I can taste it now—and then visited what the locals call "The End." Montauk is the easternmost point of the Hamptons, known for its beautiful beaches, relaxed atmosphere, and outdoor activities. We visited the historic Montauk Point Lighthouse, commissioned by George Washington, and to this day, I still have the beautiful pictures hanging on our wall at home.

I'll never forget climbing all those stairs, looking out over the ocean, when suddenly the foghorn went off and we had to come down immediately. It felt like something out of a movie.

One morning, I woke up early, drove to Sag Harbor, and parked my car overlooking the ocean. I had my iPad in hand, ready to write. Suddenly, tears welled up in my eyes as I realized this was the same place I had once come for refuge, peace, and to find myself again. Now, I was here beginning my book. It was an incredible, full-circle moment, and I felt so grateful God had given me this opportunity.

Over the next ten-plus years, I would find that the only time I could write or work on the book was while on vacation. The areas I have written in include Jackson Hole, Wyoming; Estes Park and Vail, Colorado; Isla Mujeres and Cancun, Mexico; and Taos, NM, to name a few.

WHEN LIFE TURNS SUDDENLY

Not long after that trip, life took a sudden turn.

Erik and I were at our church service for Good Friday at Klyde Warren Park in Dallas. Some of our best friends, Cindy and Dave, were in town, and we were at a restaurant that overlooked the park where music was playing. I noticed a phone call coming in from a 605 area code, but I didn't answer, thinking it was too loud and assuming it was a permanent makeup client. Moments later, a text came through: *"This is Chelsea Laine's manager, and she has had an accident."*

I couldn't believe what I was reading. I excused myself and called the number. They told me Chelsea Laine had been at work and had a seizure—something that had never happened before. And here we were in Dallas, while she was attending school in South Dakota.

After an appointment with Dr. White at UT Southwestern, we learned she had an AVM—an arteriovenous malformation—and would require three embolization surgeries and one cranial brain surgery.

There are so many details to this story, and I could write an entire book about it, but there is one moment I will never forget.

SURRENDERING WHAT MATTERS MOST

On the day of her eleven-hour brain surgery, I went into the hospital chapel, put on some of my favorite praise and worship music, and cried and prayed. Thank goodness no one else was in there at the time.

I completely surrendered Chelsea Laine to God, remembering what Paige's mom had said when her own daughter died in an accident. I prayed the same words: *God, she was Yours before she was mine, and I know You love her more than I ever could. I surrender her to You and trust You completely.*

People later said to me, "You must have been going crazy with worry," but I wasn't. I was at peace, knowing God was in control. It was a long road to recovery, but by God's grace, she healed completely and is doing great. That season taught me that even in our most powerless moments, God is still fully in control. When I placed my daughter into His hands, He gave me peace that surpassed all understanding. That kind of trust doesn't come naturall—it is built moment by moment, choice by choice, until your faith becomes stronger than your fear.

DISCUSSION QUESTIONS:

1. Is there something or someone in your life that God is asking you to surrender to Him today?

2. What would it look like to fully trust God in an area where you've been holding back?

3. How have you experienced God's peace in the middle of a difficult situation?

Devotional Scripture: Proverbs 3:5–6 — *Trust in the Lord with all your heart and lean not on your own understanding; in all your ways submit to him, and he will make your paths straight.*

Reflection: When life takes an unexpected turn, we're often tempted to cling tighter to control. But true peace comes when we release our grip and place the outcome in God's hands. Surrender isn't giving up—it's trusting the One who knows the end from the beginning and loves us more than we can comprehend.

Prayer: Father, You know the people and situations I love most, and You know how hard it can be to surrender them to You. Today, I choose to trust You completely. I place my fears, my family, and my future in Your hands, knowing that Your love is greater than mine and Your plan is perfect. Give me peace as I rest in Your promises. Amen.

CHAPTER TWENTY-FOUR

EMBRACING THE JOURNEY AHEAD

A GIFT THAT SPARKED A JOURNEY

On one of my trips back to South Dakota to take care of my permanent makeup clients, Erik and I stayed at a bed-and-breakfast in Spearfish that my sweet friend Rochelle owned, called The Secret Garden. As we were checking out, I noticed a little book on the coffee table—*The Prayer of Jabez* by Bruce Wilkinson. Something came over me, and I just knew I needed to read it. I texted Rochelle to ask if I could borrow it, and she said, "It's yours. No need to return it; just pass it on when you're done."

If you've never read this book, I highly recommend it. The simple prayer in 1 Chronicles 4:9–10 reads:

Jabez was more honorable than his brothers. His mother had named him Jabez, saying, "I gave birth to him in pain." Jabez cried out to the God of Israel, "Oh, that you would bless me and enlarge my territory!

Let your hand be with me, and keep me from harm so that I will be free from pain." And God granted his request.

This prayer—for blessing, for God's guidance, and for protection —became my own. Looking back, Rochelle's words to "pass it on" were prophetic. That simple act of giving me the book became one of the first ways I noticed God using me to reach others with His love and direction.

A PAUSE IN WRITING

One year into my marriage to Erik, I decided to sign up for Part Four of *The Road Adventure*. I had started writing the book you are now reading after feeling God nudged me to do so, but not long after, I put it aside. I wasn't sure why I had stopped until, during an exercise at *The Road Adventure*, the director asked me, "Do you know why you're not writing?"

I told her I didn't. She smiled knowingly, and after a few moments, the truth hit me—I didn't want Chelsea Laine to be embarrassed. Her gentle reply stayed with me: "She's a grown woman, and she's fine. If God brought you the idea, He will work it all out."

During this year, I was really seeking what God's will was going to look like in my life. I had read another book by Bruce Wilkinson called *The Secrets of the Vine*. Though I wasn't an avid reader, Wilkinson's books spoke to me in a special way. Being that they were short, quick reads, I could finish them quickly and have a sense of accomplishment.

I had always admired people who would say, "I read this book in a week" or "I read this book in a couple of days!" It always seemed mysterious and intriguing to me. I had grown up having trouble comprehending what I was reading, which translated to reading slowly.

I would often have to read a sentence a couple of times to simply understand what it was saying. I would also get so tired as I began to read a couple of pages. Despite these challenges, I was determined to become a better reader. Of course, I know how to read, but I wanted to dive into books like others I had known. I wanted to seek as much knowledge about God as possible.

MY FIRST 5:00 A.M. APPOINTMENT WITH GOD

The Secrets of the Vine taught me many valuable lessons that I would carry on my journey of seeking God's will for my life. One of the things it taught me was to journal. At the time, I didn't really understand it. At one point, a section of the book recommended that I wake up at 5:00 a.m. to spend quiet time with the Lord. I remember thinking, *well, that's great for other people, but I'll just start this "spending quiet time with God" stuff at 7:00 a.m.* To my surprise, the very next day, something miraculous happened.

I woke up at 5:00 a.m. on the dot. I looked over at my alarm clock and thought, *What am I doing up this early?* Then I started to smile. *It couldn't be.* For a second, I thought, *Maybe I'll just go back to sleep.* And then right away I changed my thoughts. *God allowed me to wake up at 5:00 a.m. I am rested, and this IS my appointment time with HIM. So, I'd better get up and see what He has in store for me.* Following what the book talked about, I began to journal. I had a diary when I was little, but had never journaled in the way the book was suggesting, and I didn't really know what I was supposed to write. My first entries said simple things like, *"Dear Lord, thank you for everything in my life."* Then I just started writing about my day.

The next day, I was up at 5:00 a.m. again, and the next day, and the next day. Usually, I would read a little, sometimes in my Bible and sometimes in a Christian book or devotional. Then I would pray and finally, journal. I absolutely loved how I felt! I was connecting to God in a way I had never felt before. For most of my life, I would pray at night before bed, or when I was scared or in trouble. Of course, we also prayed in church, but I had never really spent daily time with Jesus, our Lord and Savior. On day four or five of journaling, a miracle happened. I was writing, and suddenly the Holy Spirit came over me in a new way, and my pen couldn't write fast enough. It's like I was praying and journaling, and God was speaking to me, and I was just writing out His words of direction, comfort, and knowledge. Wow, it was such an amazing experience!

A LIFESTYLE OF PRAYER

This is a practice that has stuck with me for over ten years now. In the last three years, it has changed a bit, and at first I felt guilty, but now I don't and am just open to changes. I am more in a place of praying for others, meditating on God's Word, and saying my daily affirmations. Sometimes I use this time to listen to sermons, devotions, podcasts, or praise and worship music. Other times, I simply sit and rest in the presence of Jesus.

I love doing something called *Restorative Stretching*—it's similar to gentle yoga, but for me, it's really a quiet time with God. I'll put on worship music, breathe deeply, and let my body fully relax. Psalm 46:10 says, *Be still, and know that I am God* (NIV), and in those moments, I often hear Him most clearly. It's not about any other belief system—it's simply a way to release stress, keep my body healthy, and spend time in His presence.

Although it looks a little different from that in the movie, I have my own prayer room that I learned about in the movie *The War Room*. It is an area upstairs at our house where I store my books, my own comfy chair, my journal, and my essential oils and diffuser that

I turn on when I start my prayer time. I really like to bask in the scents of Cedarwood, the Three Wise Men, or Envision blends, as they are known to stimulate feelings of creativity and resourcefulness, encouraging renewed faith in the future and the strength necessary to achieve your dreams.

THE JOY OF GIVING BOOKS AWAY

These books that I started reading were so important to me and changed my life! I couldn't wait to share these books with others. I loved them so much that I began to go to Half Price Books and look in the clearance section to purchase books cheap enough so that I could give as many away as I wanted to, as God led me. A few years later, I discovered the BIG clearance sale held in a warehouse at Market Hall. I was like a kid in a candy store! I got my basket and headed directly to the Christian book section. I was picking out not only *The Prayer of Jabez* but many others I had read that were significant to my life. It was so much fun!

People would see me getting multiple copies of the same books, and they would ask, "Which ones are you looking for?" They would hand them to me when they came across them! I had been doing this for a couple of years, and an employee asked me if I was with a church. I told him that I had my own ministry, Amazing Grace Retreats, and he told me to tell the cashier, and that they would probably give me the books for one dollar! *What?!* I couldn't believe it because most of the books were $2-$5 apiece, and if this happened, I would be so grateful! I could give even more books away!

I rolled my cart up to the checkout and told the lady what the man had told me to tell her. She didn't speak, and I just kept putting books up on the counter. As we finished, she said, "The total is $256."

I said, "Ok, so are you able to allow me to purchase the books at one dollar?"

She said, "Yes!" I paid, and as I walked out to my car, I got tears in my eyes and felt like it was just the biggest blessing! God is so good, and now I have 256 books added to my collection, so I could "gift" them to anyone when God *nudges* me to!

One funny story from a sweet friend of mine named Robin, but we always called each other Sissy (from the movie *Urban Cowboy*) she would tell people, "One day when Erika and I were having lunch and we walked out to our cars, she opened up her trunk as if she was selling something and then handed me a book from a container she had in the back of her car." It was a book that came to her mind when we were talking over lunch. I thought this was a funny story, but this is what I did. I kept 20 or so books and handed them out whenever God nudged me to. This is what became of my book ministry.

That little book from Rochelle sparked something in me that has never faded. As my prayer life grew and journaling became a daily rhythm, I realized God wasn't just teaching me—He was preparing me. This wasn't just about my spiritual growth; it was about planting seeds for a ministry that would reach far beyond anything I could imagine.

DISCUSSION QUESTIONS:

1. How has a single book, conversation, or moment of encouragement impacted your walk with God?

2. What does "enlarging your territory" mean to you in this season?

3. In what ways has God used small beginnings in your life to start something greater?

Devotional Scripture: 1 Chronicles 4:10 — *Jabez cried out to the God of Israel, 'Oh, that you would bless me and enlarge my territory! Let your hand be with me, and keep me from harm so that I will be free from pain.' And God granted his request.*

Reflection: Sometimes the smallest gifts can hold the greatest impact. God delights in taking our willingness, however small it may seem, and multiplying it for His glory. The key is to respond when He nudges—because that step of obedience could change not only your life, but the lives of countless others.

Prayer: Lord, thank You for using small moments to do big things in my life. Help me to be attentive to Your nudges, willing to act in faith, and ready to share what You've given me so that Your love can reach farther than I could ever imagine. Amen.

CHAPTER TWENTY-FIVE

STEPPING INTO NEW DOORS

THE CALL TO RETREAT

B y 2014, I felt like I was ready to return to my Dallas roots. I knew the area, and it just felt more like home. I talked to Erik about it, and he was open to the change. So, we moved to downtown Dallas at Third Rail Lofts in a high-rise apartment on Main Street. It was a new adventure and I was grateful that Erik was happy, too. He had raised his boys in a suburb called Midlothian, about 30 minutes from Dallas, and had never lived in the city, so it took a bit of adjusting for him. At first, he joked that he felt like he was on vacation and wondered when he was going home.

Before long, we both embraced living the urban life in downtown Dallas. There was no yard work or driveways, just elevators to the downstairs and—boom! You're there on the street with everything close by. We soon found our favorite restaurants and became regulars. We developed friendships with several restaurant owners, waiters, and bartenders, and have attended some of their weddings, too! Since Erik and I were empty nesters, we ate at the bar area in restaurants more often than not, simply because there was usually no waiting.

This also became another part of our ministry. You meet a lot of people while at the bar. By listening to their stories, sadness, troubles, and joys of life, you can learn a lot. Then, when you feel led by the Lord—that infamous God-nudge—God shows you a way to plant a seed of His love, direction, and hope that they may have never heard explained before. I remember someone coming in and asking Erik to come outside to talk, as he had a spiritual matter to discuss. It is not our way to preach to anybody outright, but to simply love on them with words of encouragement, direction, and acceptance, hoping to plant a seed that may grow in their lives as they continue to seek God's will.

A SPA, SOME STILLNESS, AND A NUDGE FROM GOD

Shortly after we moved back to downtown Dallas, I joined the Verandah Club at the Anatole Hotel. It is not a highly frequented or advertised club, and I had actually worked there in the spa when I was 19 years old as an esthetician. I remember being amazed as my regular clients would come into the health club and spa five days a week. At the time, I just couldn't imagine being able to live that kind of life. And now here I was, decades later, living that reality!

I was in a restorative stretching class at the Verandah a few times a week and loved it. This allowed me to relax my mind and pray, plus it had excellent health benefits for my body, as well. If you know me well, you know I can't pass up a good spa! I love to be pampered, facials, massage, and any other fun treatment! I am such an extrovert and love to be with people, but quiet time away at a spa is essential. It feeds my soul and rejuvenates my mind.

One Saturday morning, I was at the Verandah, praying and meditating on God's Word, when a thought came into my mind: *Retreat.* I wondered what God meant by that, and I heard it again. *Retreat.* I still wasn't sure what it all meant, but I couldn't ignore it. Here was another *nudge.* The hardest part about seeking God's will for your life is when you feel that He is nudging you in a direction to do something out of your comfort zone; it is to be obedient. I would say that this is a learned practice. It doesn't happen overnight. It is an act of faith for sure.

PRAYING IT THROUGH

I left there that day and continued to pray and ask God what He meant by telling me that word. Did God want me to start a retreat?

Morning after morning, day after day, for the next year, I continued to seek His plans for this idea God had put in my heart. I journaled a lot during my time of prayer and sought counsel and guidance from a few spiritual mentors and friends whom I trusted. One of them was named Stacie, and she was my hairdresser at the time. She and I talked about the retreat when I was getting my hair done. She agreed that having a retreat for women was a great idea! We met on several occasions to discuss what the retreats would look like. She and I would meet at King Spa a couple of times to relax, plan, and just have fellowship. I was grateful for her friendship and input. It turns out she is a fabulous cook, and she volunteered to cook for the first retreat. She did a beautiful job! I will never forget her willingness to come and help facilitate and serve. Stacie was another confirmation that I was hearing from God. Loving the women who came to know God more closely is such a gift. This is the part that makes retreats so special.

THE FIRST AMAZING GRACE RETREAT

Soon, all the details of having a retreat fell into place. The first retreat was to take place in May 2016. I decided to kick off the inaugural weekend in my beautiful Black Hills of South Dakota, where I had lived and experienced so much healing, peace, and joy. Some of my closest friends came to support my new endeavor and take part in a relaxing, wonderful, and pampering weekend.

The first retreat was hosted at a cozy cabin near Lead, South Dakota, on a Friday evening. When the guests arrived, we had a meet and greet time and served hors d'oeuvres and refreshing drinks. This allowed everyone to get settled into their rooms and fellowship a bit. Next, we gathered together with our opening announcements, had dinner, and began our first session. Each session, I would speak on a topic such as forgiveness, and then we would talk about our experiences and areas in which to improve.

Throughout the weekend during the retreat, there are opportunities for guided restorative yoga, hiking, spa treatments, hot tub and sauna, teaching lessons, and new beginnings for each person who attends. Depending on the location, each retreat can have some variations, but the mission is the same: to offer Christ-centered retreats and workshops to help women find clarity, overcome struggles, and discover their true calling.

SERVING TOGETHER

Since 2016, we have hosted two retreats per year, one in the spring and one in the fall, in the Black Hills. As of 2021, I felt led to retire from the beauty industry in order to host more weekend retreats and workshops. And now have hosted 2 Amazing Grace Retreats at Allaso Ranch in Hawkins, Texas. In 2020, I also felt led to start the *Amazing Grace Talk Podcast*. These are easy-to-listen-to conversations with everyday people who have personally experienced the power of the amazing grace of God.

As I mentioned earlier, the book "*The Prayer of Jabez*" *was* instrumental in my growth with the Lord. Part of the prayer says, "expand my territory (or borders)." So, as I continued to seek God and how He was going to continue to expand my territory, I continued to do all of the things He was revealing to me and asking from me. In addition to the retreats, I also began hosting a few-day workshops and luncheons at the request of my dear friend, Robin.

My husband, Erik, and I were active members of Fellowship Church in downtown Dallas. We were volunteers on the greeting team, assigned to the VIPs or the first-time guests. We loved it! We loved serving together at church. When you serve and volunteer at your church, you are seeking to love God by loving others. But the miraculous thing is that God ends up blessing you in so many ways you could not even imagine unless you have experienced it. There is always a place for your spiritual gifts if you are willing to use them.

Romans 12:6 says, *We have different gifts, according to the grace given to each of us* (NIV). If this is a new term for you or you would just like to know more, then I recommend attending one of our Amazing Grace Retreats to really dive into your gifts and how you can start living them out. The Bible says we, the Church, are like a body that has many members, and each part is important. 1 Corinthians 12:12

states, *Just as a body, though one has many parts, all its many parts form one body, so it is with Christ* (NIV).

Serving others really lifts your spirit and takes the focus off your problems. It allows you time to give your worries to God instead of trying to figure out how to fix everything that is broken in your life. Proverbs 3:5-6 says, *Trust in the Lord with all your heart, don't lean on your own understanding, look to Him and He will guide your path* (NIV).

WHEN OBEDIENCE TURNS INTO OVERFLOW

Throughout the years, I continued to attend the C3 Conference that I had gone to when I previously lived in Dallas. I thoroughly enjoyed volunteering there, and even created my own volunteer role as the maitre d. I would float around between the coffee shop, wiping tables or restocking, then talking to people and getting to know their stories. It kind of became a joke that I would report to volunteer central, and when they would assign everyone to their given stations, I would say, "I've got mine!" The leader just laughed and said, "Great!" I really enjoyed making sure all of the volunteers and the guests felt comfortable and that they had what they needed.

Though I served as a volunteer, I was still able to take in the speakers and teaching sessions during the weekend. I was introduced to many of my favorite pastors and speakers at these events, including TD Jakes, Jentezen Franklin, Levi Lusko, Mark Batterson, Steven Furtik, Sy Rogers, Christine Caine and Greg Rohlinger, to name a few. The messages shared by these pastors, and many others, were so significant in my spiritual growth. As I met people who I felt could benefit from these messages, I would send them their way. I truly lived by my belief that it is only our job to plant seeds of hope. It is on the individual to receive it and God's job to grow it —we are not responsible for saving everyone or the outcome of the sharing. Just remember: when you feel the *nudge*, go with it.

Some of the messages I heard from these pastors have stuck with me since I heard them, and I share them regularly with anyone who has a need. Sharing sermons, messages, and recommending books has also become part of my ministry in spreading God's love and grace.

One year, I invited one of my best friends, Shelley Goad, to C3, and I bought us a book by one of the speakers, *Draw the Circle: The 40 Day Prayer Challenge* by Mark Batterson. We read it together, and I re-read it each and every year. I highly recommend it to help you understand more about prayer, your faith, and how believing and expecting God's favor can change your life. Since then, I have noticed that many of my pastor friends also love it and re-read it regularly as well. Maybe it's time for me to get it back out again!

Fellowship Church was great about discipling its members and offered a lot of classes to help us learn and grow. I signed up for as many as I could! I even chose to take the "University of Next Level," a college-level leadership course. We studied about Nehemiah and building the wall in 52 days. Another course I enjoyed during this time was called "High Definition Living," which is from the book *Bring Clarity to Your Life's Mission,* by Pastor Ed Young.

By 2014, Fellowship Church had grown to the point where they were launching a new campus in Highland Park Village. Since Chelsea Laine had attended middle school there and loved it, we were asked by the campus pastor, Ken, if we would like to move to that location and help start the church. Several friends of ours opted to do the same. The new church was hosted in the Highland Park Theater, a really neat location. We had to set up and tear down each week, but we had teams of volunteers who made it happen with ease. It was a lot of work for everyone; however, I will tell you it was one of the best times I can remember for fellowshipping with other couples and friends. It's truly a blessing to serve together with others.

A sweet couple, Rosangela and SamZurawel, volunteered their home for us to have a Bible study a couple of times a month. They even offered child care upstairs. The men usually gathered outside, and the women in the living room. It was really one of the most dynamic times for our spiritual growth in our marriage at that point. Great leadership and amazing friendships grew. We all valued our time together and serving at the church. Through this, I fully grew to believe that not only is attending church important, but getting involved with a small group is huge for understanding God's Word and being accountable in your growth. We were not meant to do life alone!

In 2014, Fellowship Church decided to close the Highland Park church location. We were sad, but rolled with it. Some of us went back to the downtown location, and some moved on to other churches. Many of us remain friends, even if only on social media. We all share a special place in each other's hearts. These friendships are cherished, and we will remember them for a lifetime.

Those retreats, workshops, and moments of service weren't just events—they were glimpses of God's Kingdom at work through ordinary people. And while I didn't know it at the time, He was preparing me to take the biggest leap of my career and step fully into the calling He had placed on my life.

DISCUSSION QUESTIONS:

1. When has God nudged you to step out of your comfort zone for His purposes?

2. How do you see your unique gifts making an impact in the lives of others?

3. What steps could you take to create more space for God to speak to you?

Devotional Scripture: Romans 12:6 — *We have different gifts, according to the grace given to each of us.*

Reflection: God equips each of us with gifts that are meant to be shared. When we use them in service to others, not only do we bless those around us, but we also grow in our own faith. True fulfillment comes when we align our talents with His purposes.

Prayer: Father, thank You for the gifts You have placed in me. Help me to use them for Your glory, to serve others with love, and to trust You when You call me beyond what feels comfortable. May my obedience become a testimony of Your goodness. Amen.

CHAPTER TWENTY-SIX

FROM BEAUTY TO CALLING

LETTING GO OF A LIFELONG CAREER

I continued to spend more time in prayer, seeking what God had for me next. I had been doing permanent makeup at this point for close to three decades. As I spun my client around in the chair, I heard the Holy Spirit say to me, *No more eyeliner by the time you're fifty.*

To be honest, I had felt burned out many times through the years doing permanent makeup, even though it was familiar and I was very good at my skill set. I always enjoyed my clients and booked more time than I needed to do their permanent makeup in order to offer time to talk and listen if they felt the need to tell me what was on their heart, and they usually did. I love people and wanted to be a safe place for them to share anything they needed to share. My friend Dantia, who is a hair stylist, calls it "ministry behind the chair."

Being in the beauty industry, I enjoyed the privilege of being one-on-one with clients and becoming their sounding board. Often-times, I would hear about very personal things, even before husbands or family members. I remember way back in my 20s when I listened to a client's story and bought her the book *Codependent No More*. I guess I was "doing ministry" back then, although I wouldn't have called it that at the time.

I hit a few roadblocks, as you'd expect—mostly in my own mind. Walking away from the profession I had known my whole life wasn't easy. It's hard to let go of something that's been part of your iden-tity, especially when it means starting over completely and building everything from scratch. My faith was being stretched, and I felt like I was standing at a crossroads. Do I keep doing what's familiar and ignore what God has spoken so clearly to me? Or do I take the leap, trust Him, and let Him lead me into something new?

It turns out that I did both! I spent a lot of time in prayer, journal-ing, and consulting with a few of my spiritual mentors and trusted friends. One of them was Rosalie, who was such a wonderful mentor to me. They prayed over me, prophesied over my life, and encour-aged me to fast as a Biblical key to unlock certain subjects from which I needed to hear from God. I went on my first 21-day Daniel fast (based on the book Daniel in the Bible).

As I was discussing all of this with my sweet and always support-ive husband, Erik, God started to reveal more and more of the plan He had for me. Soon, there was an open door of opportunity that I could not even imagine. When doors open and you feel peace, you can trust it is an answered prayer from God. Roadblocks are usually set up for a reason, to tempt you to go the other direction away from God's will.

One of the things that was hard about leaving my career and moving into God's perfect plan was not only leaving the income behind, but my identity in the beauty industry. After all, this is all I had known for almost 30 years. Of course, I know that what you do is not who you are. I get it, but walking through it and being obedient is a little challenging and stretches you outside of your comfort zone. Trusting in yourself and believing what God says about you instead of listening to the enemy telling you who you are and who you are not. God doesn't call the qualified—He qualifies the called.

One of my best friends since childhood, Shelley Goad, always reminds me of this verse, *But God chose the foolish things of the world to shame the wise; God chose the weak things of the world to shame the strong. God chose the lowly things of this world and the despised things—and the things that are not—to nullify the things that are, so that no one may boast before him* (1 Corinthians 1:27-29 NIV).

There is a quote attributed to Mother Teresa that says, "God has not called me to be successful, He called me to be faithful."[7]

Sometimes when I need a nudge to help me get back on course to God's plan, or when I am feeling doubt, I also remember this verse: *I can do all things through Christ who strengthens me* (Philippians 4:13, NIV).

When fear comes in, remember that it is okay to ask God questions. He likes to hear from us, whether that's joyful praise, asking questions to God, or even yelling like I had in the car so many years ago when I was forgiving the unforgivable.

A LEAP OF OBEDIENCE

The Amazing Grace Retreats grew from eight to ten people that first weekend to almost 50 at Allaso Ranch in Hawkins, Texas. In August of 2020, I finally said goodbye to my permanent makeup career. Yes, I jumped! I was finally ready for all that God had for my new journey. Some would call this a leap of faith, but I just call it obedience. So, what was next? It was time to reach out with a carefully written letter to all of my long-time clients who had become more than just clients. By this point, they were considered family, and many of them had become some of my closest friends.

CLOSING A CHAPTER, OPENING ANOTHER

As I wrote the letter, I felt a sense of closure. It was good, but it was a bit uncomfortable. I wrote and let them in on my new plan and where I felt that God was leading me. I gave them great recommendations as to who would now be taking care of their permanent makeup needs. Thankfully, anyone needing eyebrow microblading was sent to Chelsea Laine since she had been doing this for years. I really had to pray through the feeling that I was somehow letting them down. God always has a way of relieving that uncomfortable feeling if you are walking in His purposes.

I had always loved hearing people's stories of how God had moved in their lives, and the idea was born to start my own podcast. I got a referral to an amazing producer, Rob Price, who was a pastor and professor at SAGU College in Waxahachie. He taught podcasting and media and was also the author of *The Blood Covenant*.

He helped me in so many ways to start the *Amazing Grace Talk Podcast*, which has had three seasons and countless episodes of amazing God-stories with thousands of downloads on all listening platforms, including Apple Podcast, Spotify, Audible by Amazon, and more.

A few years later, I wrote my first book, *Amazing Grace Retreat Lifestyle*. This is a book about all of the ways that God healed me and helped me on my journey to freedom! (You can find more information in the resources section at the back of this book.)

Looking back, I can see how every step—every goodbye, every leap of faith, every new beginning—was part of God's careful preparation for the season I am in now. He was weaving together my story so that I could help others step into theirs. And as one chapter of my life closed, another chapter—full of purpose, healing, and divine appointments—was just beginning.

DISCUSSION QUESTIONS

1. Have you ever felt God nudging you to leave something comfortable in order to follow His calling? What was your initial reaction?

2. How can obedience to God bring peace, even when it involves letting go of part of your identity?

3. Who in your life has encouraged you to trust God's plan during times of transition?

Devotional Scripture: Psalm 37:5 — *Commit your way to the Lord; trust in him and he will do this.*

Reflection: Stepping away from what you've always known can feel risky and even frightening, especially when it has defined you for years. But God's call is never random—He sees the full picture of your life. The challenge is not to cling to the familiar but to trust that His leading will position you for something greater than you could create for yourself.

Prayer: Lord, thank You for Your calling on my life. Give me the courage to release anything You are asking me to let go of, even if it feels like part of who I am. Help me to trust that You are guiding me into something new and beautiful. Amen.

CHAPTER TWENTY-SEVEN

NEW SEASONS, NEW MIRACLES

NEW SEASONS AND LESSONS

In 2017, my dad was diagnosed with Lewy Body Dementia. As the disease progressed, I could tell that my mom needed more help, and I wanted to spend as much time with him as possible. Subsequently, Erik and I decided to move closer to my parents.

What I didn't realize at the time was that this move would also reconnect me with pieces of my past in the most unexpected ways. When we moved back to Texas, Chelsea Laine was going to check out a community college in Midlothian. We had finished the tour when, in conversation, I suddenly realized that the girl leading us was Paige's niece, Lyndsey. I said, "You're Lyndsey? You're Paige's niece?" I put my hands on her shoulders and pulled her close as if I were hugging her for Paige. I was bawling, and so was she—and even Chelsea Laine. It was a beautiful moment. I had always dreamed of this, thinking, *"If I could ever meet her, I would tell her how much her Aunt Paige loved her."* That day, God gave me the chance.

Since then, she has called me her Aunt, and she has become like family to us. I am proud to be a "stand-in" on this side of Heaven for one of my dearest friends, Paige. From that day forward, Lyndsey and I shared a bond that felt like a gift straight from her Aunt. Our connection didn't stop at that emotional encounter on the college campus—soon she began inviting us into other parts of her life, including her church.

Lyndsey invited us to Trinity a few times, and we also visited another start-up church in the area. My husband and I had graduated from high school with the pastor, and one of my childhood friends' families also attended. At first, it seemed like a logical choice for it to be our new church home. But then one Sunday, while visiting Trinity Church in Cedar Hill, my husband had an amazing God-encounter that let us know immediately that Trinity was, in fact, our new home.

I can't remember what was going on at the time, but Erik was feeling some anxiety one Sunday at Trinity Church. During the praise and worship, he felt like his legs were wobbly. I told him to just sit down. He was sitting there with his head bowed and his eyes closed when a man who had gone up for prayer at the front of the church saw that Erik was upset. He came over and sat down by him and began to speak to him. I thought, *Wow, what a sweet man he is to come over and pray for Erik, talk to him, and show comfort during this moment!* I could see him speaking to Erik, but couldn't hear what he was saying. All I could do was smell him. *Yes, smell him.* He appeared to be homeless, which was not normal for this church due to its suburban location. I began to think, *Oh no, I hope Erik doesn't miss out on this blessing because of the way this man smells.* When the man finally walked away, I asked Erik if he smelled him. He said, "No, not at all." I was so grateful. Erik's anxiety that he had when he came to church with was simply gone. It was a miracle to us as we had not understood or encountered this kind of faith in action. We formally joined the church soon after, and I swear we never saw that man again. I often wonder if he was an actual angel that God sent to give Erik a message of comfort and peace.

At Trinity, we found ourselves learning about the Holy Spirit in a whole new way! During praise and worship, we would often have a prayer team of people in twos who prayed over or for people. This was a new experience that brought so much comfort, and we loved it. We sat in the second row, mostly because I am very ADD and need to be close to the action in order to focus! But also, in my opinion, this is where you can truly feel the Holy Spirit.

Have you ever had the experience when you are listening to a beautiful praise and worship song or hear someone speaking, and complete peace comes over you? Sometimes chills? Well, that is what it feels like to be in the presence of God. I had felt it in the past at different times throughout my faith journey, but I was feeling it more and more at Trinity, and I loved it. It just made me feel so connected to Jesus and drenched in His peace.

During this time, we met some amazing people, including Cyllas and Thais Marines, pastors from Brazil who were now on staff at Trinity. Not long after becoming members, they asked Erik and me if we would like to help them lead the volunteers for greeting and first-time guests. We had a long, wonderful lunch with them to discuss our responsibilities, and said, "Yes." This is the area that we had been volunteering at our previous church, so it was familiar, and we felt called to be a part of this ministry. We felt strongly about leading others to do their best to serve God and shine His light on others, whether that was first-time attendees or long-term members. I heard from countless people that Erik was the reason they came back to the church. He was so warm and inviting and welcoming. I would often hear how he had prayed for someone, and it really meant the world to them. This made me smile and feel proud to have such a sweet and kind husband.

We also took some classes that helped us learn more about the Bible on a deeper level. In particular, we learned a lot about prophecy, deliverance, soul ties, and being baptized in the Holy Spirit. During this same time, I heard about a class through a divine appointment that taught the Raindrop Technique called CARE (Center of Aroma Research and Education).

A DIVINE APPOINTMENT WITH ESSENTIAL OILS

I say "divine appointment" because I was not actively looking for a class to take regarding aromatherapy. I was simply connecting two people I knew so that they could discuss essential oils. I dabbled in my use of essential oils, but barely. My long-time dear friend Donna was a true guru with oils; she knew every remedy, and I fully trusted her. But when I went back home after a conversation with my friend who had mentioned she was interested in trying essential oils, I tried to log on to my account and was surprised to see that I hadn't even ordered in over a year! That's how little I knew and used essential oils. I knew lavender smelled good and was used for relaxing, and Thieves was for immune boosting and fighting off viruses, but that's about it.

I called Donna to ask who might be a good point of contact for my friend to begin ordering from an essential oil company, and I tried the two phone numbers she gave me. The first was Karen, who was fairly high up in the network marketing company, and she and I had an awesome conversation. The following day, her assistant,

Jen, called me and invited me to a Center of Aroma Research and Education course. She said, "Just pray about it and let me know." As she told me what the class was about (emotional release, chemistry of essential oils, healing oils of the Bible, and the raindrop technique), I knew I just had to be there! I felt the Holy Spirit immediately and told her, "There is no need to pray about it— this class *is* an answered prayer!"

I was supposed to be at another convention the same weekend, but I felt God had told me not to buy a ticket for it. As the time got closer, I saw some friends who were going and almost caved and bought a ticket because it seemed like a fun event, but I didn't. So, when this opportunity came to me, I knew it was a sign from God. On top of it all, Jen told me that I could stay at Karen's house! What? This just kept getting better and better.

I talked to my husband and told him that I felt the need to be at this class. He said immediately, "Then you should go," and handed me the cash for the weekend. A couple of days later, I was off on a five-hour drive to Tulsa, Oklahoma, for the CARE conference.

I was excited to learn all of the information, and I soaked it in. As I learned all about the benefits of healing oils, I couldn't help but think of my daughter's throat situation. A few months prior, an ear, nose, and throat doctor in Rapid City, South Dakota, told her that she needed to have her tonsils removed. They did not give her a diagnosis or any medication, just that she needed to schedule surgery to have them removed. I was with her for that appointment, and something just didn't sit right in my spirit. Plus, she would have to lie low for two full weeks post-surgery, missing a lot of college classes, so for that reason alone, we decided not to move forward with the suggested surgery.

We decided to schedule the surgery for June instead with my ENT at Medical City in Dallas, who had performed my vocal surgery many years prior. At the end of the CARE weekend class, I asked the teacher if I could sit down and speak with her about my daughter's throat. She came up with a regimen of essential oil products, supplements, and oils that she thought would benefit Chelsea Laine. I sent it all to Chelsea Laine, and she started taking the products. Within three weeks, her throat was completely healed.[8] *What? Can this be real?!* Well, it was. After months and months of a throat that hurt and looked "like a monster," despite all odds, her throat was completely better. I was in awe. I wanted to shout it from the rooftops about the amazing healing that these products could bring.

THE POWER OF FORGIVENESS

A couple of weeks later, Chelsea Laine said, "Mom, my throat hurts." I was devastated and confused. I felt helpless. We scheduled an appointment with our chiropractor, Dr. Bo, who is not only an amazing doctor, but a healer, too! This was a divine appointment as well. God is so good when you look to Him in faith to work out your problems instead of trying to fix them all.

Dr. Bo just happened to have extra time that day. I do not remember scheduling an extended appointment, but we went into a private room and we talked. After we told him the story, he looked directly at Chelsea Laine and said, "Who are you angry with?" Then he told us that anger resides in the throat and that she needed to forgive whomever it was, and her throat would get better. Well, y'all, that is exactly what happened. To this day, if she feels a sore throat, this is her practice, along with prayer, asking to forgive the person she is angry with, and taking the supplements.

We decided to keep her appointment with Dr. Kirkham, the surgeon, for June, and guess what he said? "She was most likely misdiagnosed and probably had mononucleosis tonsillitis. If the ENT in

South Dakota had performed surgery on her at that time, that would have been horrific. She does *not* need her tonsils removed."

You may not know much about alternative medication or healing practices, but I would encourage all of you to pray about it each time you are given a diagnosis and possible prescription medications. I urge you to search your heart and ask God to guide you to learn more about natural healing practices and how our bodies were made to heal themselves. A good reference book is *Healing Oils of the Bible* by David Stewart, Ph.D., and *Feelings Buried Alive Never* Die by Karol K. Truman, and *The Pathway to Emotional Healing* by Jennifer McCraw. These books will expand your thinking and could even save your life physically and emotionally. And please check out the podcast on Amazing Grace Talk, "From a Runner to a Wheelchair to a Miracle by Tina Hansen." Her testimony shows that God will restore us if we do the emotional and spiritual work.

People are so quick to believe and have faith in traditional doctors before praying or using their own common sense. It doesn't help that every other commercial is advertising a prescription for this or that. Sometimes, even if you are really healthy like I am, you stop and think, *Do I have any of these symptoms? Which is what Big Pharma wants people to think.* In my research, I have found that most of the time, physical ailments come from emotional issues that have never been resolved.[9] Keeping our emotions buried deep in our minds can lead to collateral damage later in life, which can cause physical problems. Anxiety, sleeplessness, bitterness, unforgiveness, and more can cause a lot of physical and mental problems. Don't let fear or limiting beliefs hold you back from true healing for you and your entire family for generations to come. Satan comes to kill, steal, and destroy (John 10:10), and often tries to leave us trapped in generational sins. But God is bigger than generational curses.

There is power in words at many levels. Our words can shape a person's identity and self-image so that they consistently act in ways that confirm their beliefs about themselves, whether positively or negatively. But there is also something prophetic about our words that call realities into being.

I remember years ago, I called a long-time dear friend of mine who had her PhD in psychology and asked her this question: "Isn't anxiety simply caused by emotional issues not dealt with?"

I remember a long pause on the other end of the phone, and then she said, "You are exactly right."

I have always been able to discern specific things that people are going through, and now with our online life coaching programs, Amazing Grace Retreats, we are able to help women move from a past that they want to leave behind to the life that God intended for them. It is the best feeling. I say that I am a lifelong learner, and I always encourage myself and others to stay attentive and stay tuned in for what is next. You will be amazed at what you are able to accomplish and where life takes you!

My mother also believes in the same principles to this day. As I write this book, she is 85 years old and rarely takes prescription medication. She is very active and plays senior Olympic pickleball and basketball. She actually just finished her tenth Senior Olympic Games. She exercises regularly and eats pretty healthy, other than some good ol' southern or German cooking. My father lived to be 89, and except for the last three years of his life with Lewy Body Dementia, he was healthy and strong. When the doctors would tell my mom or dad that they would need to be on medication for the rest of their lives, she would say, "No, we will not!" She would always seek prayer and an alternative solution.

This even was true when I was a child, and I suppose I've always had this deep-seated philosophy of natural healing in me due to that.

When we wouldn't feel well before school, she would say, "Well, tell yourself you feel good and you will—then get up and get going!" So many times, the way we feel physically is about perspective and attitude. Of course, this tactic doesn't work 100% of the time, but it does more times than not.

CIRCLING BACK TO THE PRAYER OF JABEZ

Let's circle back to that infamous book that so touched my life, *The Prayer of Jabez*.

Jabez called on the God of Israel, saying, "Oh that you would bless me indeed, and enlarge my. Territory, that Your hand would be with me, and that You would keep me from evil, that I may not cause pain!" So God granted him what he requested (1 Chronicles 4:10 NIV).

Many people I have come across have never read this Scripture in the Bible. Many do not feel worthy to ask God to bless them. They have even told me that they feel selfish praying for God to bless them. *The Prayer of Jabez* was a miraculous part of my spiritual journey and really launched me into motion for ministry. It is my privilege and honor to share it with others, and I do so on a daily basis. This remains one of my most-gifted books of my book ministry to date.

Ask and it will be given to you. Seek and you will find: knock and it will be opened to you. For everyone who asks receives, and he who seeks finds. And to him who knocks it will be opened (Matthew 7:7-8 NIV).

God will arrange circumstances and opportunities that are more strategic for you. It will be as if God has become your master scheduler. You won't get more hours in the day, but you will discover more effective ways of using the hours you're given. The Holy Spirit will show you the way. When you feel that *nudge*, listen and walk in that direction. You just have to be open to change and growth.

INVITING YOU TO STEP INTO YOUR OWN CALLING

Although my journey has been difficult at times, it has opened my eyes to God's love and His amazing grace—and for that, I am forever grateful. My hope is that my story encourages you to reach out, receive His love, and experience His grace so you, too, can discover the purpose He has for your life.

I would also like to personally invite you to read *The Prayer of Jabez* and my first book, *Amazing Grace Retreat Lifestyle*, and to consider signing up for the next Amazing Grace Retreat. It is a time set apart to refresh, recharge, and realign so that you can live fully—not only for your own life but for those you love most. Remember the familiar airplane analogy: in an emergency, you must put on your own oxygen mask first. The same is true in life—we can only be our best for others when we first care for ourselves.

DISCUSSION QUESTIONS

1. Can you recall a "divine appointment" in your life where God arranged circumstances in a way you could not have planned?

2. How has God used an unexpected person or situation to encourage or comfort you?

3. What role does forgiveness play in emotional and physical healing?

Devotional Scripture: Romans 8:28 — *And we know that in all things God works for the good of those who love Him, who have been called according to His purpose.*

Reflection: New seasons often require new levels of trust. God may use unexpected moments, encounters, or even strangers to reveal His care and direction. His miracles are not always dramatic—sometimes they come as a quiet answer, a healed body, or a moment of peace when you least expect it.

Prayer: Father, thank You for the new seasons You bring into my life. Help me to see Your hand at work, even in the smallest details. Give me eyes to recognize Your miracles and a heart ready to forgive, so that I may walk in Your fullness. Amen.

EPILOGUE

MOVING FORWARD

As I look back on my life, I can distinctly see God's presence guiding every decision and breakthrough along my journey. Throughout this path, I've felt many gentle nudges from Him, encouraging me to share my story to inspire and encourage others. There's a deep joy in helping people!

Right now, I have the privilege of doing this through my umbrella company, The Amazing Grace Lifestyle, which was born from the inspiration and support of my close friend, Ginny. Over the last three years, The Amazing Grace Lifestyle has thrived, largely due to my partnering with ShelleyJane, who has been an incredible source of strength for me. God knew exactly what I needed to fulfill His plans and purposes for my life, and I am profoundly grateful that He united us to share His love and grace in ways I never imagined, helping women navigate their journeys with newfound empowerment.

Within our organization, I founded the Amazing Grace Retreats, hosted in the Black Hills of South Dakota since 2016, and at the Allaso Ranch, a beautiful retreat center in Hawkins, Texas. In 2020 I started a podcast produced by Rob Price, Amazing Grace Talk that shares uplifting stories of faith and transformation, (you can find it on YouTube or anywhere you listen to a podcast) complemented by a coaching platform dedicated to helping faith-filled women recover and heal from past relationships so that they can attract their God given, husband they have only dreamed about. We're also proud to have established Amazing Grace Ministries, a 501(c)(3) nonprofit. Our mission is to support single mothers and their children who are facing crises by offering faith-based inner healing, addiction counseling, financial classes, and basic legal advice. We also offer day retreats and events to serve and love single mothers.

It is my sincere aspiration to follow the Divine guidance from God to help other women find their way to freedom and fulfill their God-given purposes. For more information about our initiatives, please check the resources section of this book.

Throughout my life's journey, I've come to realize that genuine healing and wholeness go beyond just overcoming pain and granting forgiveness. They involve stepping into the person I was always meant to be. This is my anthem of redemption, and it can be yours too if you're ready to welcome it. I encourage you to embrace the Amazing Grace Lifestyle alongside me.

Over the years, God has turned every fractured part of my journey into a beacon of hope for others. The Lord has transformed what the enemy intended for harm into a compelling testimony. This testimony has developed into something I could never have imagined back then.

I am currently at the helm of The Amazing Grace Retreat Lifestyle, a retreat dedicated to helping women find healing, renewal, and the courage to embrace the future. Planning these retreats is not just about coordinating events; it embodies the very core of my ministry.

When women arrive, I can often perceive the weight they carry—some have just weathered a storm, while others are still grappling with one. From the moment they cross the threshold, my team and I strive to create a safe haven for them. Soothing music envelops the space, and the scent of essential oils in a diffuser lingers in the air. Every detail is purposefully curated to convey a message: you are seen, you are valued, and you are not alone.

Each day finds a perfect balance between teaching, worship music, and restful reflection. Mornings begin with quiet contemplation and guided prayer, flowing into sessions where we read God's Word and connect it to the challenges we face in our daily lives. Afternoons take on a more leisurely pace—walking through the grounds, journaling by the fire, or sharing stories over a cup of tea. I've learned that healing often unfolds in these peaceful, unstructured moments just as much as it does during our formal gatherings.

One retreat stands out in my memory, particularly because of a woman who shared her story with us. She came on the insistence of a friend, arriving with no expectations, but with an unspoken pain hidden deep inside her. On the second evening, as we participated in worship, she was overcome with emotion and quietly confessed, "I didn't know God could love me like this." This moment served as a profound reminder of my purpose—highlighting the importance of every detail—because when God's love touches a hurting soul, true transformation happens.

On the last morning, we gather in a circle, our hands linked together, and our voices soft but filled with hope. Each woman takes a turn sharing a truth she will hold dear, while we bestow blessings upon one another. Amidst the tears, a sense of joy permeates the space, reminding us that this moment is not an end, but a new beginning in our journey with God. My prayer is that this retreat becomes a wellspring of strength they can revisit in their hearts whenever they feel overwhelmed by life's challenges.

Looking back on my journey, I understand that each season of my life—filled with both challenges and victories—has been preparing me for this purpose. These retreats are more than just a weekend experience; they aim to empower women to embrace a lifelong journey of freedom and grace that God provides. It fills me with immense joy to see them leave feeling lighter, stronger, and with a renewed sense of confidence in their identity in Christ.

One thing I know for sure is that God never lets anything go to waste. Every tear you've cried, every obstacle you've encountered, and even the errors you've made—He has the power to turn them into something meaningful. My hope is that you recognize the deep truth that you are incredibly loved, fully forgiven, and entirely equipped to pursue the life God has designed for you.

Friend, if you are ready to take the next step toward healing and walking in your God-given purpose, I would be honored to walk alongside you. Whether it's through The Amazing Grace Lifestyle podcast, our retreats, coaching platform, or the outreach of Amazing Grace Ministries, there is a place for you here. You don't have to do this journey alone—come join me, and let's discover together the freedom, restoration, and abundant life God has waiting for you. I would love for you to join me in living the Amazing Grace Lifestyle.

GRATITUDE AND ACKNOWLEDGMENTS

To everyone who has been part of our story—whether for a single chapter, the whole book, or as we walked through healing and restoration—please know that your presence has been a gift I will carry for the rest of my life. I know you lifted us up in prayer, encouraged Chelsea Laine and me, then and now, and for that I am forever grateful.

Writing this book has been one of the hardest things I have ever done. Because of the emotional weight of my story, I could rarely write at home, where the memories were too close. Instead, God gave me the gift of writing while away in quiet, healing places. Some chapters were written in Estes Park, Colorado, where I found comfort in the same mountains I had visited as a child. Others came to life in Vail, Colorado, and Jackson Hole, Wyoming—peaceful, breathtaking settings that gave me room to breathe and reflect. At Zoetry, a small boutique hotel in Isla Mujeres, Mexico, I found rest and inspiration. In South Dakota, at The Secret Garden Bed & Breakfast in Spearfish, I discovered a fresh perspective. And more than twelve years ago, I began this work in Sag Harbor, New York—the very place where I once found refuge. Each location was not about luxury, but about finding the peace I needed to face the memories and put pen to paper.

I am grateful for all the people God has placed in my life!

FAMILY

- My parents, Rudy & Kay Seamayer
- My sisters, Ann & Karen Seamayer
- Jimmy Edwards, Darrin, niece and nephew, Alex & Nicholas Ross
- My niece, Lyndsey Anthony—what a gift from God that we were able to meet!
- Cousins Kay & Carmen Pulley, The Kuhn's, Megan Collins, Noralee Lewis, and extended family.

FRIENDS WHO CARRIED ME

- Mrs. Peggy Whigham, Julie Doyle & Tim, Stella, Oscar, & Julius DeLaughter
- Jason Litt, Mark Pirro, Bryan Wakeland, Shan Stan Gann, Sandy Repka. Thanks for all of the love and the school lunches!
- Sabrina, Steve, Cassie, Jessica & Savannah Askin
- Jerry & Suzanne DeLaughter, Heather Davis & Rolyn Barthelman
- Anji & Ricky Raitt, Julie Brady, Michelle Assunto
- Corky Randolph, Randy Stewart, Greg & Melanie Henke
- Robert & Kellie Fancher, Charlie & Denise McMullin, Jason Swivels
- Christopher Martin, The Fashion Plate!
- Becky & Brett Hudechek, Shelley Goad, Kim Clab
- Lesly & John Swilling, Nonie & Darren Jones
- Dantia & Chris Tate, Beto Pena, Jackie Pena, Keith Ozment
- Kim Shockley, Tish & Guy O'Brien

- Darlene & Larry Fornicola, and all of the girls at Hair Logics
- Tim & Diane Klesmit, Andy Kawamura, Jeremy Boss (aka Foxy Arms), TJ Martin
- Nicholas Mezzour, Steve McPhearson, Randy Melancon, Robin Raetzman
- Kristi & Rand Blair, David & Michelle Broussard, Kevin & Kim Batista
- Irma & Anthony Turrubiartes, Ken & Tiffany Kalloor, Rachel & Ryan Maynard
- Donna Shivers, Michelle Esposito, Tyler Wentz
- Aeriel & Alexis Miranda, Carvena Harris, Monique Stone, Ursula Walker, Hillary Barr
- Lawrence Mendive, Kyle & Marisa Turner, Bill Reeves, Patty Howard, Cydney Skeens, Rachel Bingham, Eric Culbertson, Bobby Le, Teel Tishgart, John Wilson
- Polly Rea O'Toole, JD & Linda Cantu, Susan Stacy, Tammy & Yuki Nakamura
- Dorota van der Merwe, Ma~Monique, Sean Edison Chankersingh, Andrea Purcigliotti, Andrea Nappi,
- All of our friends at Thorntree Golf Club

CLIENTS WHO BECAME FAMILY

- Amy Turgeon, Bo Parker, Shelley Casino, Michelle Runyan, Michael Horowitz, LuAnn Ericsson
- BethAnn Spracklin, Ellen Chernoff Simon
- I have so many special clients who meant the world to me but just cannot name them all. You know who you are and I will forever be grateful that God put you in my life.

CHURCH & MINISTRY FAMILY

- Pastors Ed & Lisa Young and all of our Fellowship Church family
- Pastor Jim & Becky Hennesy, Minister Barbara Walker
- Galen & Della Wilson, Monica Vessa, Ana Onorato, Karla & Dallas Evans, Miriam & Tommy Evans, Melissa & Anthony Medina
- Fanny Minnitt Ministries and all my friends at Trinity Church
- Kirsten Johnson, Monica & Danny Blevins, Sabrina & Field Harrison
- Jim & Beverly Johnson, and our board members for Amazing Grace Ministries.

LIFELONG ENCOURAGERS

- Ginger & Phillip Traughber, Earnestine & Shane Ransom
- Linda & Jonathan Cooke ("Mama & Daddy said fast!")
- Cathy Barnes-Gaberdiel, the teacher who believed in me.
- JoConda "Mama Jo" & Papa Mick Dana, Nicole Dana, Monique Dana Tetrault, Raquelle & Eric Strawn
- My South Dakota Sisters: Sonya & Chris Donovan, Sam & Randy Finkbeiner, Shannon Rochel, Lynette Jaskela
- Belinda Christman, Mindy Ladner, Cindy & Dave Balt
- Carolyn Stansberry & Troy Johnson, Rochelle Berg, Dana & Ron Sneesby
- Hortencia Saavedra, Dylan Roan, Pastor Keaton & Bishop Fudge

- Chelsea Laine's late husband Nick
- Stacie Richie
- Vicki Furnish, Sherrie Feist, Rosalie Torok, Lynan Formby, Tonya Booth, Sylvia Williams, Karen Saffle, Lydia Newman, and so many more who stood by me.
- If you were not named please forgive me, and know that you know who you are and you are loved all the same.

SPECIAL THANKS

- To ShelleyJane—your edits, prayers, and encouragement carried me through the most complex parts of writing.
- To Ginny Baker—your creativity and love have been constant through more than one book.
- Dylan Roan
- To Lisa Fahey—my publisher who believed in my story enough to make this miracle happen. Thank you for your guidance and inspiration.

ENDNOTES

1. https://www.theroadadventure.org
2. https://www.thequestlife.com
3. Beattie, Melody. Codependent No More.
4. The Secret. "The Secret Documentary - Digital Stream | the Secret - Official Website." *The Official Website of the Secret*, 17 Jan. 2025, www.thesecret.tv/products/the-secret-film-digital-stream.
5. "32 Powerful Bible Verses About Emotional Healing." *Faith on View*, 29 Mar. 2025, www.faithonview.com/bible-verses-about-emotional-healing/#:~:text=Psalm%20147:3%20Reflection:%20This%20verse%20portrays%20God,touch%20in%20our%20times%20of%20emotional%20distress.
6. *The ROAD Encourages, Equips and Empowers People to Live Life to the Fullest – at the Road, Shift Happens.* www.theroadadventure.org.
7. Teresa, Mother, and Brian Kolodiejchuk. *Mother Teresa: Come Be My Light: The Private Writings of the Saint of Calcutta.* 2007, ci.nii.ac.jp/ncid/BA84426111.
8. ★The personal testimonies of healing and use of natural practices and essential oils is not intended to be medical advice. Always consult with your physician regarding any and all medical treatments and protocols.
9. The personal testimonies of healing and use of natural practices and essential oils is not intended to be medical advice. Always consult with your physician regarding any and all medical treatments and protocols.

ABOUT THE AUTHOR

In 2016, Erika Seamayer-Williams founded Amazing Grace Retreats in the Black Hills of South Dakota to create a safe place for women to rest, heal, forgive, and fellowship with like-minded believers. Her passion has always been to help women find clarity, overcome struggles, and discover their true calling in Christ. Over the years, this vision has grown into a ministry that continues to touch lives through retreats, events, and one-on-one encouragement.

In 2020, God opened the door for Erika to launch the *Amazing Grace Talk Podcast*, produced by Rob Price. Through it, she shares inspiring stories of faith, healing, and victory, highlighting the power of God's grace in the lives of everyday people. Since then, she has written her first book, *Amazing Grace Retreat Lifestyle* (May 7, 2022), which tells the story of how God has brought her through challenges and equipped her to help others walk in freedom and victory with Him.

The ministry now includes the Amazing Grace Retreat Lifestyle with personal coaching. Erika helps women who have tried everything on their own to heal, move forward, and find love—yet keep ending up stuck. She walks alongside those ready to break out of dead-end cycles and step into their God-given purpose and the love they've been praying for.

In addition, the ministry offers a VIP Membership, and in 2023 Erika and ShelleyJane founded *Amazing Grace Ministries*, a 501(c)(3). Their mission is to bring hope and healing to single mothers and their children in crisis situations. They help "bridge the gap" by providing support, a healing process, and guidance through biblical principles.

RESOURCES

www.theamazinggracelifestyle.com

or

www.erikaseamayerwilliamson.com

Podcast

www.ingramcontent.com/pod-product-compliance
Lightning Source LLC
Chambersburg PA
CBHW051610120626
46551CB00014B/1741